Feeling Good with Essential Oils

Your Guide to Using Oils for Emotional Well-Being

FDA Disclaimer

Table of Contents

Why Essential Oils for Mood Support?

"Essential oils do not just cause sensory impressions, but they also alter the way in which the sensory organs themselves operate...This leads to one of the most radical ideas of modern aromatherapy: by altering the way in which sensory impressions are perceived and transmitted to the brain, essential oils ultimately alter what we consider to be real. This means that essential oils can change how we see the world--they can change our worldview. This can be of the highest significance for true healing."

Kurt Schnaubelt, p116 (The Healing Intelligence of Essential Oils)

Introduction

Welcome to *Feeling Good With Essential Oils*! We're so excited to have you join us on this journey!

We want to assure you that, whatever the emotional struggle you are seeking support for, there is hope!

We created this book for the person who was looking for an easy-to-use handbook on essential oils for emotional support, that was backed by scientific data, and mixed with the personal experiences of others. This book takes a practical approach and stance on using essential oils and gives you the knowledge you need to help yourself move from a state of negative emotions into a neutral or positive emotional state. We wanted this to be a highly functional book that allows you, the reader, to take the complex experience of emotion and turn your experience into a positive breakthrough simply by utilizing the essential oils you have in your home.

If you are using this book to help yourself: We believe YOU are the expert on you and your body. We're here to give you some insight into how to use plant-based medicine to help you feel your best. Take these protocols as guidelines to serve and support you, but if you're not keen on an aroma or a blend, then move onto the next one that calls out to you. There are no essential oil police that will come and tell you you're using the wrong oil blend. If it makes you feel better--then it works for you!

If you are using this book to help someone you love: We highly recommend getting their consent **before** trying to resolve their emotional state. By all means, DO feel free to diffuse some oils in the air around them that correspond to their emotional state or struggle. Diffusing oils around them may very likely help create an environment of a more positive and agreeable state of being. But if your goal is to have them pull through a deep emotional condition or negative emotional state, you will need them to acquiesce to using the protocols listed in this book. People have to *want* to heal. It's important to gain their buy-in with moving forward beyond their own struggles. We cannot do the work for them, but we can partner with them. Offer your support to them by diffusing a few oils or offering a loving massage with a few oils that correspond to their struggle.

What You'll Find in This Book

Oils and Blends Recommended:

Here we include an array of essential oils that help support moving beyond an emotional ailment or emotional state of distress. Fear not, you do not need to have all of these oils--but if you do, great! Use them! Start with what you do have on hand and utilize the recipes to navigate what feels best in your body.

Protocols:

Try them all, try one, try a few--it's up to you! Do note: Many of the protocols in the pages of this book include "aromatherapy inhaler blends." This is where an oil user makes a custom blend by pouring 2-4 different oils onto a cotton-wick diffuser and placing it into an aromatherapy inhaler tube. Instead of simply recommending water or hand diffusions, we have focused on protocols using inhaler blends because aromatic inhalation is one of the most effective and potent ways to positively impact one's mood. With aromatherapy inhalers you can create an easy, portable, long-lasting aroma that can be enjoyed regularly on-the-go. Whereas with water or hand diffusions you are contained to one room with a diffuser or having to pour oil onto your hands for a hand diffusion every time you want to experience the benefits of that oil. Our aim is to provide you more freedom and flexibility as you use your essential oils aromatically. But if you love your diffuser or prefer hand diffusions, you're welcome to do those instead of making an aromatherapy inhaler.

Suggested Duration:

Everyone's life experiences, situations, and circumstances are different. Use the recommended durations as a guidepost to follow a path that feels good to you. You may need to use the oil protocols a little longer than recommended or for slightly less time. However, the longer you use them, be regular and be consistent (set reminders on your phone, create a ritual to set up your diffuser for the day after your shower, or tie your new aromatherapy habit to an established one by taking a whiff of your inhaler every time you take a drink of water). You may also find that once you move through one primary emotion (like Anger) another secondary emotion (perhaps Sadness, or Embarrassment, or Fear) will pop up that was hiding underneath that initial layer of emotion. When that occurs, you may need to make a transition to begin a new protocol that corresponds to the secondary emotion and make that your new focus.

Additional Recommendations:

Because everyone's body is different, unique, and holds their own stories and histories inside of their DNA, each person has the potential to experience essential oils for emotional support uniquely. In fact, research suggests that for some people their gender and race will influence their affinity to certain oils and aromas.[1] This section gives you variances for trouble-shooting protocols, alternating aromas, and inspiring creativity in designing your own protocol. Have fun with it! If you're not feeling very creative, we've laid out the recommendations for you. But if you feel like thinking outside the box, take these guidelines and create your own blends. Most importantly, do not give up! If something doesn't work for you the first time—simply try the next protocol.

Testimonies:

We have done our best to share relevant stories and testimonies to help you connect with these oils and oil protocols. We hope these stories touch your heart and fill you with hope.

Individual Oil Reference Sections & Oil Blends Reference Sections:

Here you will learn a little bit about each oil, or each blend, individually and what they are generally used for, or good for using per their chemistry. This section can be thumbed through over a period of weeks or months as you become curious about each oil one at a time or it can be consumed in one sitting while you sit back with a favorite beverage in a cozy spot. Either way, enjoy learning all about the awe-inspiring and wonderful world of essential oils and their ability to help transform emotional patterns and states. We hope you come out of this experience transformed, renewed, and inspired.

Three Ways to Use Essential Oils for Supporting Emotions

As you begin to embrace the practice of using essential oils for your mental health journey or the journey of someone you love, there are three primary ways essential oils are used that you will want to familiarize yourself with: aromatic, topical, and internal use.

Aromatic: This is where the aim of utilizing an essential oil is to inhale the tiny microscopic chemistry and molecules that make up the essential oils, receiving the effects of the essential oil's chemistry via the olfactory system of the body. This is considered one of the most effective ways to utilize essential oils

for regulating emotional states.

Examples of aromatic use:

» Placing a few drops of essential oil into a diffuser reservoir with water and inhaling the aromatic mist

» Placing a few drops of oil into the palms of your hands, cup your hands over your nose and mouth, and deeply inhale for 4-5 breaths

» Sprinkling a few drops of oil onto cotton-wick inhaler or a lava stone-style diffuser jewelry to inhale periodically throughout the day

Topical: This is where the aim of utilizing an essential oil is to place the oil strategically on a location of the body, organ, spine or acupressure point that corresponds to the ailment. The majority of oils may be best utilized neat, while others may be best utilized diluted. Some oils may even need to be applied carefully to certain areas of the body that remain under clothing as they can become "phototoxic" in the sun (See section on Essential Oil Safety). What is so great about topical application is that often when applying the oils to the body, the user will still receive the aromatic benefits of the oil as well.

Examples of topical use:

» Applying a few drops of oil to your chest, wrists, back of neck, spine, bottoms of the feet, etc. or anywhere on your body

» Applying strategically to acupressure points, over certain

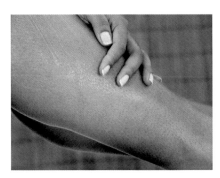

organs, or via caressing touch and massage

Internal: This is where the aim of utilizing the essential oil is to get it into the body via intestinal or sublingual absorption. In this book, you will see examples of internal use recommendations in the "Additional Suggestion" section of protocols most often because internal use is usually a secondary support to aromatic use in emotional ailments. If a condition is extreme or chronic, it may require internal use of essential oils or other essential oil-infused supplements.

Examples of internal use:

» Drinking 1-2 drops of oil in a glass of water
» Placing a few drops in a vegetable capsule and swallowing
» Using essential oils in food, beverages, or condiments

Essential Oil Safety 101

Essential oils are basically containers of highly potent distilled plant matter. Therefore, when it comes to safety while using essential oils,hey are generally just as safe as if you were using an herb or flower in your kitchen for cooking. Essential oils are *extremely* potent. Just one drop of Peppermint oil is equivalent to 28 cups of peppermint tea. *(Mmmm...minty!)*

The general rule of thumb for using essential oils is to start small and increase the drops you use as needed from there, slowly. If a protocol in this book recommends more than 1 drop **internally**, you can start with 1 drop first then slowly add more until you reach the full protocol recommendation over the course of a couple days. However, if a protocol in this book recommends 2-3 drops **topically** or **aromatically**, you can confidently begin with these amounts.

Use both common sense and your intuition to guide you with essential oils.

When we say "Use common sense" we mean: Never put an oil directly in your eyes or directly into ear canals. Also, do not place oils undiluted onto sensitive areas of the body like your genitals.

When we say, "Use your intuition to guide you" we mean: If before you bought this book, you know that you are someone who is very sensitive to many things in the world (chemicals, allergies, medications, smells, etc.) then start with smaller amounts of essential oils and increase to full protocol amounts in the book. Give yourself time to acclimate and calibrate as you go.

Most essential oils are very mild and safe for undiluted contact with most skin types, and none of the oils or blends recommended in this book are considered harmful or dangerous by any means. However, when it comes to the delicate membranes in our eyes, ears, and genitals we generally want to avoid contact with them.

Phototoxicity: A short list of oils fall into the "Phototoxic" category. This means they react with the sun and can cause a severe sunburn-type reaction to the skin when the oils are applied topically and then a person immediately goes out into the sun. When using phototoxic oils on parts of the body exposed to the sun, be sure to stay inside for the day, or cover the areas you applied oils to with a shirt, pants, or hat, or simply apply these oils to body parts that will stay covered and remain out of the sun.

List of Phototoxic Essential Oils Mentioned in This Book: Bergamot, Wild Orange, Grapefruit, Lime, Lemon, and Tangerine leaf (though Tangerine rind is generally not considered phototoxic).

Basic Safety Tips:

» Start small with 1 drop and work your way up to multiple drops

» When in doubt, dilute before applying to skin

» Children under 6 years old, pregnant women, and the elderly have much more delicate skin, so diluting the oils or using a pre-diluted rollerball version of an oil is recommended (like the Kids line, Touch line, or Emotional Aromatherapy line)

» Keep phototoxic oils or blends that contain phototoxic oils off your body parts that will see the sunshine that day

» When pregnant, avoid using oils such as Clary Sage or Jasmine as they can impact hormones

Dilution: How much should I dilute?

Most of the blends in this book are pre-diluted and safe for use with most skin types. If you'd like to make your own rollerball blends or dilute before applying to children, elderly, or sensitive skin here are some guidelines.

As a general rule of thumb, children under 6 should have a 1-3% dilution, between 6-12 should have a 1.5-5% dilution, children between 12-17 should have a 1.5-20% dilution, and elderly or sensitive skin should have a 1-3% dilution.

10ml Rollerball with 2 drops essential oil = 1% dilution

10ml Rollerball with 4 drops essential oil = 2% dilution

10ml Rollerball with 6 drops essential oil = 3% dilution

10ml Rollerball with 10 drops essential oil = 5% dilution

10ml Rollerball with 40 drops essential oil = 20% dilution

Evasive Essential Oil Mishap Tips:

If you experience an unpleasant reaction or sensation from using essential oils topically on your skin, wash with a mild soap and then follow-up with wiping the area down with a carrier oil on a tissue (such as coconut oil, fractionated coconut oil, olive oil, jojoba oil etc) to absorb remaining oil and soothe irritation.[2]

In the event that you get an essential oil accidentally in your eye, it should be flushed with a liquid carrier oil (not water) such as fractionated coconut oil to carry out the essential oil from the eye and surrounding membranes.[3]

Laying the Foundation For Health

This book will guide you through protocols that you can apply to your unique array of emotions. These protocols are natural, but powerful. They work with your body to support what it was intended to be: well.

Besides the specific protocols you will be able to apply to your unique emotional array, however, we want to give you some information on "foundational supports" that are for everyone, every day. They will help the oil protocols work even better!

Science shows the rise in emotional issues is often multifactorial. That bears repeating. It is multifactorial. We are built with enough resilience that it generally requires several hidden underlying causes (missing "foundational supports") for us to become symptomatic. More specifically, research indicates *it takes only four out of the known 10 hidden underlying causes to overwhelm the emotional reserves of most people.*[4] For additional information about the hidden causes you can go to: nedleyhealthsolutions. com.

Below are the 10 hidden underlying causes. Assess yourself with the underlined questions as you read each one to see if you have more than four hidden underlying predispositions to emotional unrest.

1. Genetics. Many of us have been told our issues are genetic if we have a family history of the problem. This is not a truly accurate way of determining genetic predisposition. For instance, when people with major depression have actual genetic testing done, most of them do not have the genes we think may be related to depression. Genetics account for only 10-20% of our predisposition to physical and emotional diseases. For example, if we take a person from rural China and transplant them into America, their risk for degenerative diseases and emotional problems that are plaguing America soon start to catch up to those of the people they are living around. In other words, much of what is plaguing us is due to our lifestyles. That's good news! We can fix lifestyle easier than our genetic code!

2. Lifestyle. There are lifestyle supports for our emotional health that have a powerful impact, for better or worse, depending on if they are present or absent. How do you know if you have a problem with your lifestyle? <u>Do you exercise at least five days a week, for at least 30 minutes, and do you get at least 30 minutes of sunlight (or bright light from a light box if living in a colder climate) a day, and do you do some deep breathing once a day?</u> If you answered yes, you're doing well! If you answered no, there's work to do.

Let's start with exercise. *Brisk* walking (at least three miles per hour) will work, but increased benefit will come from "intermittent training" where you will walk (or jog, if your level of fitness allows) for 30 seconds and then jog (or sprint, if you were already jogging) for 40 seconds, walk for 30 seconds, jog for 40 seconds, repeating. Intermittent training helps us get in shape faster than just walking or jogging alone, so you can actually get your minimum amount of exercise done in only 20 minutes with intermittent training rather than 30 minutes of brisk walking. It also has the added benefit of supporting your thyroid function. 30 minutes of brisk walking is the absolute bare minimum and can be used as a "maintenance" level of exercise. If you're actively struggling emotionally, however, an hour of brisk walking should be the minimum, daily. *Expect* to be sore when you start. But even if you're only starting with 10 minutes of walking a day, keep it up! Consistency is the key. Also, having a partner to exercise with will greatly increase your chances of sticking with it. Accountability, more than ability, will get you to your goal.

Despite your age or current level of fitness, science shows that we have remarkable inherent resilience and ability to improve. One woman who started an exercise program was in a wheelchair, unable to walk more than ten steps without great pain. One month later, having started with the ten steps she could handle the first time, and working up from there, she was out of the wheelchair, eventually walking ten miles a day. For issues like depression and anxiety intense exercise can have almost an immediate effect in reducing symptoms. Work with your doctor if in poor health while getting started, but do start.

You need sunlight to produce serotonin. Take those sunglasses off for a little bit (wearing a wide-brimmed hat for sun protection still works) so your eyes are exposed to sunlight and you can make that important neurotransmitter. Sunlight sets our internal body clock, so *when* you get your sunlight is important. It's best to get 30 minutes of sunlight right upon awakening, before 7 A.M., to help set your clock and stop insomnia. If your struggle is with early morning awakening, get an additional 30 minutes of sunlight in the afternoon, before 4:00 P.M. If you live in a dark, cold climate, a light box can be a great way to get your sunlight

(indoor light is not sufficient however). If using a white light box, get a 10,000 LUX box. If getting a blue light box, get a 460 nm wavelength box (this is the wavelength of the blue sky). With a blue light box, you can decrease your light exposure from 30 minutes to 20.

Getting sunlight exposure is especially helpful for those who overeat, for "winter depression," and for postpartum depression. It also regulates hormones for women with irregular cycles and for men with erectile dysfunction. The sun is important to your physical and emotional health!

Science shows that taking time to breathe deeply is more important than previously realized. For instance, one form of well-studied deep breathing, Sudarshan Kriya Yoga (SKY), helped 73% of people suffering from Generalized Anxiety Disorder who were non-responders to medication and 41% of them had a full remission of anxiety. SKY is easy to learn, try breathing in for five seconds, then out for five seconds. You can take these long, deep breaths as you're showering, or while lying in bed counting sheep. Aim for at least 20 minutes of deep breathing daily.

3. Circadian Rhythm (Sleep/Wake Cycle). How do you know if your emotions are being negatively impacted by your circadian rhythm? <u>Do you get between 6-9 hours of sleep a day and do you get at least one hour of that sleep before midnight?</u> If you answered no, we have work to do.

We need to sleep in a completely dark, quiet room (white noise like waves is OK, but TV or radio is not) and some of the sleep needs to be before midnight. Why? Those are the ideal conditions under which your body makes melatonin, a hormone regulating stress hormones and immune function. We can also improve our sleep by turning screens off by 8:00 P.M. Viewing a glowing screen disrupts our sleep patterns. For instance, in one study participants read an electronic book rather than a print book before bed. This delayed sleep by about ten minutes, decreased REM sleep and resulted in reduced morning alertness.

4. Nutrition. Poor nutrition is the most common hidden

underlying problem for people suffering from depression and/or anxiety. Also, for those who are "non-responders" to medication, it's often the missing part of the equation. *Medications will not overcome nutrient deficiencies that undermine emotional wellness.* How do you know if nutrition is an issue for your emotional well-being? <u>Are you on a whole food, plant-based diet?</u> If you said no, your nutrition is likely negatively impacting your brain's function. Why? *Animal foods have what we call "competing amino acids" that stop many nutrients that help build neurotransmitters from making it to our brain.* While there are numerous books on the subject of healthy food, there is wide discrepancy among them. What to trust? We recommend a book written by a medical doctor who donates the proceeds of his book to charity to avoid conflict of interest, *How Not To Die* by Dr. Michael Gregor. He does a great job of summarizing nutrition research and what has been validated. We do not get any money from him for saying that. Just get it on Audible and listen to it while you drive. Or read it if you're old school and like books like the one in your hands. But go get it.

In the meantime, here are a few ways to start eating healthier:

1. Eat a *raw* fruit or veggie before every meal (nutrient value decreases with cooking). This will increase the enzymes in your stomach to help digestion of the meal and also help you feel fuller faster, since your body got the most nutrient dense part of the meal (the raw fruit/veggie) first.

2. Only. Drink. Water. Not flavored water. Just. Water. OK, a slice of lemon or some lemon oil in there will be fine, but you get the gist. Drink *at least* eight 8oz cups a day (more if you're a heavier person, exercising, or it's hot).

3. Know that when you go to the store you *need* to flip the box around and read the label before you put it in your cart. Caregivers, you especially. The primary caregiver dictates about 90% of what the family eats.. And what are you watching for on that label? If your ancestors weren't eating it 200 years ago (or 500, or 1000, or 5000 years ago) then you shouldn't eat it now.

Your body will recognize it as a toxin (because it is) rather than food and an inflammatory response is launched by your immune system. So if you see hydrogenated oil, corn syrup, or artificial colors/flavors/sweeteners, put the "food" (term loosely applied with many items at your local store) back on the shelf. Walk away. And why no artificial sweeteners? Research shows you will gain *more* weight by going with the "sugar free" or diet version of that drink. Why? The level of sweetness on your tongue signals to your body to grab onto fat! Artificial sweeteners are many times sweeter than sugar. Thus, people tend to gain *more* weight when drinking diet drinks than regular drinks. Avoid all this by sticking to water!

4. Plants, plants, plants! A whole-food, plant-based diet is one that is minimally processed and made of plants. This can be easier to do than you think. Keep your favorite recipes but make sure you're creating them with healthy ingredients without the items mentioned above (hydrogenated oil, corn syrup, artificial colors/flavors/sweeteners). Meat is easy to substitute by adding in more veggies or tofu. Research from Loma Linda has shown the *#1* thing you can do to lose weight is to simply remove *all* meat from your diet.[5]

5. **Toxins.** There are toxins in everyday household items that could be causing a hidden cause of emotional stress. Do you drink from plastic water bottles (switch to glass!)? Do you use anything with "fragrance" on the label (soap, lotion, laundry detergent, deodorant, etc)? Do you use personal care products with sodium

lauryl sulfate, sodium laureth sulfate, cocamidopropyl betaine, polysorbates, polyethylene glycol (PEG) or phenosyenthanol in them? This list is far from comprehensive but if you're not sure about an ingredient on your product, look it up at ewg.org. Remember, what you're breathing in or slathering all over your body better be safe enough to ingest because it does make it into your body! When we throw new chemicals into the complex biochemistry of our bodies, we cause hormonal changes that impact both our physical and emotional health.

Worth mentioning here is the "odd condition" person. If that's you, and you know who you are ("I've been to ten doctors and they just don't know what's going on..."), run a check of your current medications to see if they may be an underlying factor. You may be dealing with a side effect of a medication. Go here to check your medications to see if the side effects are the "odd condition" you've been dealing with: drugawareness.org.

One last thing we just have to mention on this topic because we know a lot of you are moms — become educated on immunizations. Please learn the other side of the story so you can make an informed decision for your family. Watch *Vaxxed*, or *The Truth About Vaccines*. There have been no studies on the safety of the currently recommended vaccine schedule.

6. Social Support/Major Loss. Life is complex. There are situations we encounter that can have both negative and positive impacts. Here are some questions to help you discern if your recent experiences are likely impacting your mood. Within the last six months, have you been through any severely stressful events? Within the last 18 months have you had a major loss, such as loss of a loved one, health, or a job? Are you responsible for raising grandchildren? Is your income inadequate for your basic needs? Do you lack close relationships or do you have a close relationship with an abusive person or someone who suffers from addiction or mental illness?

If what we are dealing with is a major loss, it's important to recognize there are tasks to grieving that will support you in the journey. To support ourselves as we mourn loss, we must first accept the reality of the loss. At this stage it's important to communicate about the loss. A mourning ritual (funeral or memorial) is also important if the loss was a loved one.

Second, work through the pain. Some may want to use medication as a support but these can often bring complications of their own. Be honest about your feelings and maintain social and spiritual ties, even if tempted to withdraw. Poor social support during a major loss is more predictive of developing long-term depression (rather than situational depression from the impact of the loss) than if you'd been tortured. We are social beings; not islands.

Do your best to continue with good self-care, and write, write, write your memories. Writing helps to take the loss from the occipital (visual) lobe to stop the "movie" that can turn to PTSD. At this stage, watch out for "should've, could've, would've, if only... " statements regarding the loss. They are not productive and only increase hurt.

It's important to evaluate how you are doing emotionally *month by month* as you mourn your losses. If you find you are not improving month by month, seek a counselor who can assist. Also, if you are in a relationship that is abusive, seek counseling. Many who are consistently unhappy in their relationship have not even realized it's abusive. Defining problems, and then finding solutions that allow forward progress while accounting for complex considerations can be a balancing act that requires support. Cognitive Behavioral Therapists who focus on giving tools that find solutions can be very helpful. If you want a checklist of tools for emotional support to start with immediately, we recommend *Your Happiness Toolkit* by Carrie Wrigley.

7. Addiction. Do you use illegal drugs, use tobacco or view pornography? Do you consume alcohol more than once a week or benzodiazepines (Xanax, Klonopin, Librium, Ativan, etc.) more than twice a month? Do you have any behavior that feels "compulsive," including gambling, eating sugar, or "zoning out" in front of a screen (computer, video games, TV or phone)? Besides these addictions, others can be prescription drugs, cutting, caffeine, and social media. You can spot an addiction by a compulsion to continually use it, a need for increasing amounts, withdrawal symptoms at discontinuance, and the tendency for it to have a negative impact on your life (relationship or work problems).

To overcome addiction, it's best to abstain completely from the addiction in the same way someone addicted to alcohol needs to avoid it. Moderation does not apply to some things (say, smoking). In fact, you are more likely to overcome an addiction if you give up more than one unhealthy substance at a time. Why? Addictions tend to run together, acting as triggers for one another, like alcohol and cigarettes for instance.

When you're feeling drawn to engage in an addictive behavior, you can take a "contrast shower" where you get the water about as warm as you can stand it then turn it to cold for 30 seconds, warm for 30 seconds, then alternate again until you have had three, 30-second exposures to cold. End on the cold. These showers can be done daily. They will stimulate your frontal lobe and are also *very* helpful for depression and anxiety.

Addiction is a situation you will need support with. Research shows the most effective supports have spiritual content that encourages relying on a higher power for increased strength such as the 12 Step Program. For anonymous (online) daily addiction support, visit candeobehaviorchange.com.

8. Medical Conditions. There are many medical conditions that will negatively impact you emotionally, such as Hepatitis C, traumatic brain injury, cancer, Parkinson's Disease, diabetes, sleep apnea, Lupus, or autoimmune diseases. It is critical that you have a very thorough medical evaluation done so you do not have untreated medical conditions that are impacting you emotionally. For instance, the top symptom of hyperthyroidism (too much thyroid hormone) is anxiety. And one of the top symptoms of hypothyroidism (too little thyroid hormone) is depression. Far too many people have been told they had depression and anxiety when they were actually suffering from adrenal gland or thyroid disease.

Here's a clue you're in this category: *the problems get worse over time.* If you are worse today than the first day you sought help, you didn't get the right help. Start on a different path today by getting an updated check of your thyroid function at your doctor.

9. Thoughts/Frontal Lobe Support. It's a two-way street: Your thoughts impact your brain's healthy wiring, and your brain's health impacts your emotions and thoughts. Let's start with thoughts. *Don't believe everything you think.* It's critical we are, *daily*, watching our internal dialogue for truth. Here are some cognitive distortions (lies), with examples, that can be very undermining to our thought processes, based off the excellent books, *Telling Yourself the Truth* by William Backus and *Feeling Good* by Dr. David Burns. <u>Do any sound familiar?</u>

» All Or Nothing Thinking: Looking at things in absolutes (black or white). "If I don't get straight A's, I'll never get into college."

» Overgeneralization: Seeing a negative event as the constant pattern. "I never win!"

» Mental Filter: Dwelling on the negatives and filtering out the positives. When someone brings you cookies, you think, "These are just going to make me fat!"

» Disqualifying the Positive: Finding reasons positives don't apply to you. When complimented on losing weight, replying, "I'm still huge though."

» Jumping To Conclusions: Predicting things will turn out badly. "I'm not calling them because they will probably just be annoyed."

» Fortune Teller Error: Mind reading that others think badly of you. "She probably hates me."

» Magnification or Minimization: Blowing things way out of proportion. "This light takes forever to turn green!"

» Emotional Reasoning: Using your emotions to create facts. "I feel overwhelmed, therefore, this situation has no good solution."

» Labeling and Mislabeling: Identifying yourself or others as being their mistakes. "I ate that whole quart of ice cream. I'm a pig!"

» Personalization: Blaming yourself or others for mistakes. Watch for "should, could, would" statements. "I should've been stricter with my child when I was raising her. Then she wouldn't have these problems."

Our thoughts tend to go a certain direction given time and like ruts developing in a road it gets harder to shift out of that ravine. Just like we have muscle memory that makes repetitive acts, like driving, easier over time, the same thing happens with our thought pathways. Try this exercise to gain an awareness of your distortions and to start a new neural pathway for your thoughts. Say only positive things for two weeks. If you slip up, your two weeks starts over. You'll soon find the lure to say something negative is outweighed by the desire to not start over. Be creative in how you respond to difficulties in a positive way. Then watch for miracles.

Besides our thoughts, science shows that there's more impacting our brains, specifically our frontal lobe which is the seat of spirituality, morality and the will. Virtually all people who have depression show decreased blood flow to the frontal lobe of the brain and will start to see the impact of this in their lives. How do you know if that could be you? Do you watch more than two hours of entertainment TV/movies/video games per week? Do you

spend more than two hours using the internet for entertainment a week (social media)? Do you spend less than ten minutes a day reading for inspiration (reading poetry or scripture)? Do you engage in the practice of meditation/prayer less than once a day? Do you often go against your own conscience? Are you listening to classical music for at least 30 minutes a week? Are you using alcohol, nicotine, illicit drugs or benzodiazepines? Are you getting 5-10 fruits and vegetables a day to supply your brain with the nutrition it needs? Incredibly, all these things are impacting the function of your brain, which can have serious downstream effects. Recent research from Boston Children's Hospital has shown that those with Autism Spectrum Disorder have unique brain wave activities that finally can be used to give an accurate, early biomarker for the disorder.[6] In other words, our loved ones on the spectrum are not being helped by screens that alter brain wave activity.

Remember, screens are addictive to the brain. Expect no small amount of resistance as you decrease their use in your home. But it will be worth the increased frontal lobe function! Replace time used on screens with classical music and books, including those that inspire (this, again, improves the frontal lobe).

Meditation can be supportive of the frontal lobe, and prayer has been shown to be a powerful form of meditation. No matter our spiritual background, our brains seem to be wired for quiet daily devotion and contemplation.

10. Early Development. <u>Were you raised by anyone other than both biological parents? In childhood, were you the victim of serious abuse (sexual, emotional, violence, etc.)?</u> We cannot go back in time to change our past. However, what we focus on grows, and sometimes we must change our focus to growth. We still have choice. We can become something we don't like, let it continue to eat at our life, or we can learn and grow. As mentioned earlier, this may require some assistance. Again, be sure to look for a counselor who will assist you in meeting goals of growth, working for a finite time together (rather than developing a long-term relationship) where you will learn tools that enable and empower. You are bigger than anything that has happened to you.

Those are the ten foundational supports (hidden underlying predispositions). Did you see four or more areas to improve for yourself or a loved one that is struggling? If so, you're likely experiencing some unwanted emotions. We are so excited for your journey to begin! Get started today by picking a foundational support to improve and find an oil protocol in the following pages to go along with it!

Section 1

Emotional Ailments and Oil Protocols (A-Z)

Abused

Oils and Blends:

Basil, Pink Pepper, Cedarwood, Clary Sage, Eucalyptus, Fennel, Frankincense, Helichrysum, Jasmine, Juniper Berry, Lavender, Rosemary, Lemon, Lime, Magnolia, Melissa, Neroli, Patchouli, Roman Chamomile, Rose, Spearmint, Spikenard, Turmeric, Wild Orange, Ylang Ylang, Comforting Blend, Restful Blend, Joyful Blend

Supplements:

Restful Complex Softgels

Additional Support:

Try adding 1 drop Melissa oil to thumb and pressing to roof of mouth for 30 seconds. Try sprinkling 2 drops each of Ylang Ylang, Spikenard, and Helichrysum onto cotton-wick inhaler and inhale deeply multiple times per day (refresh oils often). Or place 1 drop of each oil in hands and inhale deeply. Diffuse 2 drops Rosemary and 3 drops Juniper Berry to inhale during therapy sessions. Apply 2 drops each of Juniper Berry, Rosemary, and Patchouli onto cotton-wick inhaler and inhale deeply multiple times per day (refresh oils often). This aromatherapy inhaler blend may be useful to use while in therapy sessions or while journaling then reprocessing event. Diffuse Joyful Blend. Take 1-3 capsules Restful Complex Softgels 30 min before bed.

Protocol

» Alternate 4-6 drops Restful Blend then 5-6 drops Frankincense in diffuser throughout the day and place diffuser in close proximity to you.[1]

» Apply Comforting Blend or Restful Blend over the heart and deeply inhale aroma for 5 breaths.

» Sprinkle 2 drops each of Clary Sage, Roman Chamomile, and Pink Pepper onto cotton-wick inhaler and inhale deeply multiple times per day (refresh oils often).[2] Or place 1 drop of each oil into palms and inhale deeply.

» Take 1 drop of Turmeric oil internally in vegetable capsule twice daily with meals.

» Apply Jasmine, Magnolia, and Neroli to the spine, to the back of the neck, or bottoms of the feet.[3]

» Diffuse 2 drops each of Wild Orange, Lime, and Spearmint.[4]

Suggested Duration:

Use daily for 3 months. Continue to use any protocols that feel supportive of positive mood state.

Addiction

Oils and Blends:

Black Pepper, Cinnamon, Geranium, Rose, Ylang Ylang, Lime, Bergamot, Fennel, Rose, Juniper Berry, Rosemary, Detoxification Blend, Respiratory Blend, Clary Sage, Eucalyptus, Spearmint, Comforting Blend, Renewing Blend

Supplements:

Detoxification Softgels, Fruit and Veggie Drink, GI Cleansing Complex, Probiotic Complex, Vitality Supplement Trio

---

Additional Support:

Try adding in Detoxification Softgels twice daily. Use GI Cleansing Complex for 10 days, then Probiotic Complex for 10 days, then back to GI Cleansing Complex for 10 days, finally finishing off with taking Probiotic Complex daily until bottle is gone. Take 1 scoop of Fruit and Veggie drink daily in the morning. Take Vitality Supplement Trio twice daily to support ongoing healthy immune system, brain, and getting daily antioxidants. Diffuse Bergamot and Lime.

Protocol

» Diffuse 1 drop Geranium, 1 drop Ylang Ylang, 2 drops Rose for healing the heart and promoting a sense of approval, love, and connection to self.[5] A person may also find 1 drop of each of these oils mixed with fractionated coconut oil and rubbed into the back, neck, and shoulders can be very soothing.

» Sprinkle 4 drops Cinnamon and Black Pepper onto cotton-wick inhaler and inhale deeply multiple times per day or per hour (refresh oils often).[6] Or place 2 drops of each oil in diffuser and sit near the diffuser. This can be very helpful for quitting smoking.

» Diffuse 4 drops Lime, 2 drops Clary Sage, 2 drops Juniper Berry, and 2 drops Rosemary for awakening the mind and inducing good feelings.[7]

» Sprinkle 4 drops each of Fennel, Spearmint, and Eucalyptus onto cotton-wick inhaler and inhale deeply multiple times per day or per hour (refresh oils often). Or place 1 drop of each oil into the palms and inhale deeply. This can be very helpful for quitting smoking or for replacing any unwanted addictive behavior with a new habit.

» Apply 2 drops Detoxification Blend applied to the bottoms of feet.

» Apply Comforting Blend or Renewing Blend over the heart.

Suggested Duration:

Use protocols for 3 months minimum. Continue on with any protocol that continues to serve and support you. User may find it helpful to move on to healing other emotions as well after using this protocol for a time.

ADD/ADHD

Oils and Blends:

Rosemary, Black Pepper, Peppermint, Lemon, Grapefruit, Frankincense, Geranium, Cardamom, Focus Blend, Kid's Focus Blend, Reassuring Blend, Restful Blend, Kid's Restful Blend

Supplements:

Vitality Supplement Trio, Energy & Stamina Complex, Fruit and Veggie Drink, Children's Omega-3, Children's Chewable

Additional Support:

Try adding in the Vitality Supplement Trio twice daily for adults. For kids, add in the Children's Chewables and Children's Omega-3 daily. Both children and adults will also benefit from Fruit and Veggie Drink in the morning. For adults struggling with symptoms of lethargy from ADD, use the Energy & Stamina Complex once daily.

Protocol: With Symptoms of Hyperactivity

» Diffuse 4-5 drops Reassuring Blend.

» Apply Focus Blend or Kid's Focus Blend to back of neck, massaging thoroughly at base of hairline into the brain stem.[8] May also apply down spine for extra boost.

» Apply Restful Blend over heart.[9]

» Sprinkle 4 drops Frankincense, 2 drops Geranium, and 3 drops Cardamom onto cotton-wick inhaler and inhale deeply multiple times per day (refresh oils often). Or place 1 drop of each oil in palms and inhale deeply.

Protocol: With Symptoms of Fatigue or Exhaustion

» Sprinkle 2 drops each of Rosemary, Lemon, and Black Pepper onto cotton-wick inhaler and inhale deeply multiple times per day (refresh oils often).[10] Or place 1 drop of each oil in hands and inhale deeply.

» Apply Focus Blend or Kid's Focus Blend to back of neck, massaging thoroughly at base of hairline into the brain stem.

» Diffuse 2 drops Peppermint, 2 drops Rosemary, 3 drops Grapefruit in morning or during peak hours of needed focus and productivity.[11]

Suggested Duration:

Use daily ongoing as needed. These two protocols are wonderfully supportive and can be used ongoing for as long as needed.

Aloof

Oils and Blends:

Basil, Rosemary, Thyme, Ylang Ylang, Wild Orange, Peppermint, Grounding Blend, Joyful Blend, Invigorating Blend, Encouraging Blend, Inspiring Blend, Captivating Blend

---

Additional Support:

Try diffusing 3 drops Thyme, 4 drops Wild Orange, 2 drops Ylang Ylang. Inhale Basil directly from the bottle for 5 deep breaths.13 Apply Captivating Blend to wrists. Bring Cypress oil into the shower and once skin is wet, apply 1 drop to top of each foot then rub into skin working up towards calves and legs. Increase to 2-4 drops, working further up the body but careful to avoid inner thighs or genitals.

Protocol

» Diffuse a mix of 3 drops each of Joyful Blend and Invigorating Blend.

» Apply Encouraging or Inspiring Blend over the heart and breathe deeply 5 times.

» Rub 3-4 drops Grounding Blend on bottom of each foot.

» Apply 3 drops each Peppermint, Rosemary, Basil onto cotton-wick inhaler and inhale deeply multiple times per day (refresh oils often).[12] If you don't have an inhaler place 1 drop of each oil in hands and inhale.

Suggested Duration:

Use as needed when emotional experiences present themselves, or use daily first thing in the morning as a preventative and diffuse/use aromatherapy inhaler as well as throughout the day.

Anger

Oils and Blends:

Lavender, Frankincense, Lemon, Peppermint, Roman Chamomile, Bergamot, Geranium, Rosemary, Grapefruit, Orange, Comforting Blend, Renewing Blend, Courage Blend

Supplements:

Vitality Supplement Trio, Fruit and Veggie Drink.

Additional Support:

Try applying Courage Blend over the heart. Diffuse either the Comforting or Renewing Blend instead of the above recipe. Take Vitality Supplement Trio twice daily to support whole-body health. Anger can be very degenerative to a person's body and, depending on how long someone has been angry. They could need the extra support of vitamins, minerals, and antioxidants so try a scoop of Fruit and Veggie Drink to support them.

Protocol

» Diffuse 2 drops each of Grapefruit, Wild Orange, Lemon, and Bergamot.[14]

» Apply 1 drop each of Peppermint and Geranium over the heart.

» Place 1 drop of each Frankincense, Roman Chamomile, and Lavender in palms and inhale deeply.

» Inhale Peppermint or Rosemary directly from the bottle to reboot and refresh the mind.[15]

Suggested Duration:

Use as needed, or daily for up to 1 month if anger is chronic. Continue using any methods above that support moving beyond feelings of anger and onto a secondary emotion that may need healing (like sadness, fear, shame, guilt, etc).

Alzheimer's

Oils and Blends:

Clove Bud, Coriander, Cinnamon, Cardamom, Lemon, Grapefruit, Roman Chamomile, Sandalwood, Basil, Frankincense, Grounding Blend, Patchouli, Wild Orange, Cellular Complex Blend, Restful Blend, Kid's Restful Blend, Uplifting Blend

Supplements:

Cellular Complex Softgel, Restful Complex Softgel

Additional Support:

Try diffusing 2 drops Coriander, 2 drops Basil, 2 drops Lemon for a mentally energizing aroma.18 Diffuse 2 drops Cinnamon, 3 drops Wild Orange and 3 drops Cardamom for neuroprotective effects.[19] Diffuse Uplifting Blend. Apply 1 drop Patchouli to back of neck and thoroughly rub into the brain stem. Take Restful Complex Softgels 30 min prior to bed.

Testimony/Story:

"My mother was 10 years into her Alzheimers diagnosis, growing more agitated and restless each day, when we first discovered oils. Once we started applying oils such as Restful Blend and Patchouli on the back of her neck and diffusing Frankincense or Roman Chamomile her mood states began to completely shift. She loves getting her hands massaged with oils now and will sit still and smile. The oils give us the huge gift of being able to support her this deep into her diagnosis when there is not much else we can do to make her comfortable. We are so grateful for these oils." - Rebecca N.

Protocol

» Apply Restful Blend or Kid's Restful Blend on back of neck to relax and ease any feelings of anxiety (Kid's Restful Blend has more delicate scent if aroma is too strong for person).[16]

» Diffuse 2 drops Clove Bud, 6 drops Grapefruit, 2 drops Roman Chamomile for relaxing, uplifting, and neuroprotective properties of blend.[17]

» Take 2 Cellular Complex Softgels twice daily for brain support.

» Massage 1 drop each of Frankincense and Sandalwood into hands and gently massage entire hand on finger pads, back of hand, and palms. This is relaxing and soothing for those struggling with Alzheimers (May also use Grounding Blend for this).

» Apply Grounding Blend to bottoms of feet and over heart.

Suggested Duration:

Use daily to support the ongoing use of oils that are neuroprotective, uplift the mood, and relaxing the central nervous system.

Annoyed

Oils and Blends:

Basil, Clary Sage, Coriander, Lavender, Frankincense, Lemon, Juniper Berry, Peppermint, Roman Chamomile, Bergamot, Geranium, Rosemary, Grapefruit, Orange, Comforting Blend, Renewing Blend, Invigorating Blend, Captivating Blend

---

Additional Support:

Try sprinkling 2 drops each of Basil, Clary Sage, and Coriander onto cotton-wick inhaler and inhale deeply multiple times per day (refresh with new oils every 5 days). Or place 1 drop of each oil in palms and inhale deeply. Diffuse Invigorating Blend to ease the mind. Apply Captivating Blend to wrists. Rub 1 drop each Geranium and Juniper Berry on the back of the neck.

Protocol

» Diffuse 2 drops each Grapefruit, Wild Orange, Lemon, and Bergamot when feeling irritable, emotional tension, or annoyed.[20]

» Apply Comforting Blend or Renewing Blend over the heart and deeply inhale 5 breaths.

» Place 1 drop of each oil, Frankincense, Roman Chamomile, and Lavender in palms and inhale deeply.[21]

» Inhale Peppermint or Rosemary directly from the bottle to reboot and refresh the mind.[22]

Suggested Duration:

Use protocols immediately when feelings of annoyance or irritability come up. Use ongoing daily until feelings dissipate. Continue to use any methods above that feel supportive and uplifting to you.

Anorexia

Oils and Blends:

Lime, Black Pepper, Clary Sage, Rosemary, Thyme, Jasmine, Ylang Ylang, Wild Orange, Magnolia, Peppermint, Grounding Blend, Joyful Blend, Invigorating Blend, Encouraging Blend, Renewing Blend

Supplements:

Vitality Supplement Trio, Fruit and Veggie Drink

Additional Support:

Try adding Encouraging Blend over the heart. Diffuse 3 drops each Thyme, Wild Orange,Ylang Ylang, while eating. Use 1-2 scoops daily of Fruit and Veggie drink to support getting vital nutrients into the body. The Omega's in the Vitality Trio will help with brain function.

Protocol

» Apply Renewing Blend over heart and deeply inhale for 5 breaths.

» Sprinkle 2 drops each of Black Pepper and Lime onto cotton-wick inhaler and carry with you, inhaling deeply for 5 breaths multiple times per day (refresh with new oils every 3-7 days).[23] This blend helps stimulate appetite and research shows that Black Pepper helps with swallowing.

» Diffuse 3 drops each of Joyful Blend and Invigorating Blend.

» Rub 3-4 drops Grounding Blend on bottom of each foot.

» Place 1 drop of each Peppermint, Rosemary, Clary Sage in palms and inhale from hands. Can be done every 1-2 hours if needed.

» Apply Magnolia to wrists/neck as a perfume to calm nerves.

Suggested Duration:

Use daily as needed to support transitioning to and solidifying healthy habits.

Anxiety

Oils and Blends:

Clary Sage, Bergamot, Wild Orange, Cypress, Frankincense, Lemon, Lime, Grapefruit, Tangerine, Neroli, Rose, Lavender, Roman Chamomile, Reassuring Blend, Restful Blend, Grounding Blend, Invigorating Blend, Joyful Blend

Supplements:

Omega Supplements

Additional Support:

If you're not yet seeing the results you'd like, try applying Rose over heart and Neroli on back of neck. Try adding different citrus oils you have to your diffuser, or inhaling them from the palms of your hand. Research shows that citrus oils are a wonderful aid in reducing feelings of anxiety.[26] Try experimenting with diffusing different citrus oils like Lemon, Lime, Grapefruit, Tangerine, Bergamot, Invigorating Blend, or Joyful Blend to achieve the results that feel best in your body.

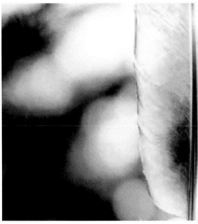

Testimony/Story:

"I used to have terrible feelings of anxiety and doom come out of nowhere. It was terrible because I would be out and about with friends or with my family when suddenly I felt the need to run away or like I was going to have a heart attack. When I started using Restful Blend over my heart and Grounding Blend on my wrists or feet, and then deeply inhaling the residual oils left on my hands, it totally changed my life. I could feel the anxious feelings drain right out of me and instead a sense of calm would replace it. I am so grateful for these oils!" - Sarah M.

Protocol

» Apply 1-2 drops Reassuring Blend to palms of hands and deeply inhale for 4 breaths.

» Apply 1-2 drops Restful Blend over heart and on the back of the neck.[25]

» Apply 2-3 drops Grounding Blend to bottoms of feet and wrists.

» Sprinkle 2 drops Clary Sage, 2 drops Bergamot, and 4 drops Wild Orange onto cotton-wick inhaler and inhale deeply multiple times per day (refresh oils often). Or place 1 drop of each oil in palms and inhale deeply.

» Diffuse 2 drops each of Cypress, Lavender, Frankincense, and Roman Chamomile throughout the day.

» Take Omega Supplements twice daily.

Suggested Duration:

2-3 months or until feelings of anxiety subside. Use one or more of the methods mentioned above as needed.

Apathy

Oils and Blends:

Blue Tansy, Lemon, Cypress, Juniper Berry, Peppermint, Marjoram, Rosemary, Clary Sage, Ginger, Detoxification Blend, Joyful Blend, Encouraging Blend, Renewing Blend

Supplements:

Detoxification Softgels

Additional Support:

Try bringing Cypress oil into the shower and once skin is wet, apply 1 drop to top of each foot then rub into skin working up towards calves and legs. Increase to 2-4 drops, working further up the body but careful to avoid inner thighs or genitals. Apply Encouraging Blend on bottom of both big toes. Apply Joyful Blend or Renewing Blend over the heart.

Testimony/Story:

"My husband's difficult upbringing, along with some key grief experiences, leave him feeling 'stuck' sometimes. These, along with a genetic "nature-v.-nurture" piece, have left him with a huge apathetic streak in his personality that is an ongoing challenge. Blue Tansy in the diffuser at night has turned out to be the most powerful tool in our toolbox to help him move through these down times! When he's feeling this way we diffuse Blue Tansy a few nights in a row (It's great for sleep!), and within a few days he 'comes alive' again, gaining back his spunk . . . getting out to work in the yard, offering to cook supper, or tackling a house project he couldn't even "see" just a few days earlier. A year ago he even found a weight loss program that appealed to him and released almost 60 pounds, something I never imagined he would have had the gumption to do, before his experiences with Blue Tansy!" - Sunny F.

Protocol

» Diffuse 1 drop Rosemary, 2 drops Cypress, 2 drops Lemon, and 2 drops Peppermint to revive the mind.[27]

» Apply 2 drops Detoxification blend on stomach above the navel to create movement in the body.

» Sprinkle 3 drops Rosemary, 3 drops Ginger, 3 drops Juniper Berry, & 2 drops Clary Sage onto cotton-wick inhaler and inhale deeply multiple times per day (refresh oils often). Or place 1 drop of each oil in palms and inhale deeply.[28]

» Take 1-2 Detoxification Softgels twice daily to promote clearing and cleansing internally to get energy moving in the body.

» Diffuse 2 drops each Blue Tansy and Lemon throughout the day or when feelings of intense apathy are present.[29]

Suggested Duration:

Use daily for 1 month or longer if needed.

Autism Spectrum Disorder

Oils and Blends:

Lemon, Wild Orange, Neroli, Bergamot, Magnolia, Lavender, Frankincense, Sandalwood, Reassuring Blend, Grounding Blend, Restful Blend, Focus Blend, Kid's Restful Blend, Kid's Grounding Blend, Kid's Focus Blend, Kid's Courage Blend

Supplements:

Digestive Enzymes, Probiotic Complex, Children's Probiotics

Additional Support:

Try applying 2 drops Sandalwood, 1 drop Bergamot, 2 drops Magnolia, 2 drops Lemon (or Wild Orange) onto cotton-wick inhaler and inhale deeply multiple times per day (refresh oils often).[32] Or place 1 drop of each oil in palms and inhale deeply. Can be done every 1-2 hours if needed. Take Digestive Enzymes with meals to help with digestive issues that are often concurrent with Autism/Aspergers. Take Probiotic Complex twice daily or for kids take one Kid's Probiotic Complex once daily.

Testimony/Story:

"Frankincense and Copibia down the spine every night has been a game changer for our son with autism. He would stay awake at night very stressed out and keep everyone else in the house up too. The oils help him to settle down and we notice that it helps him in the day too. We diffuse Frankincense with the Grounding Blend daily to help him with his anxious feelings too." -Jeff H.

Protocol

» Diffuse 5-7 drops Frankincense daily and ongoing throughout the day.[30]

» Apply Grounding Blend or Kid's Grounding Blend down the spine and on the bottom of the feet.

» Apply Focus Blend or Kid's Focus Blend to back of neck, massaging in thoroughly at base of hairline into the brain stem.

» Apply Restful Blend or Kid's Restful Blend over heart. You may also choose to diffuse this by itself or combine 2-3 drops with Frankincense in diffuser protocol above.[31]

» Apply Kid's Courage Blend around navel and on chest during moments of fearfulness or uncertainty.

» Note: Those with Autism/Aspergers may be more sensitive to aromas than others. Be mindful to start with small amounts first or allow them to smell first and "approve" of the aroma. You may also choose to use the Kid's Blends listed in these protocols for both adults and kids as they are pre-diluted and have a softer aroma that may be appealing and comfortable for some to use here.

Suggested Duration:

Use daily for ongoing support as needed. Diffuse oils all day on a continual basis to set the tone for good emotional support. Choose one or more of the above protocols to do daily as ongoing support to fit your needs.

Bereavement

Oils and Blends:

Melissa, Marjoram, Rose, Frankincense, Lemon, Geranium, Neroli, Cypress, Respiratory Blend, Comforting Blend, Renewing Blend, Centering Blend

Supplements:

Restful Complex Softgels

Additional Support:

Try adding 3 drops Cypress to cotton-wick inhaler along with 3 drops Melissa, 2 drops Marjoram, and 2 drops Geranium. Diffuse 3 drops each of Frankincense, Lemon, and Cypress during the day. If experiencing "heaviness" over chest, apply 2-3 drops Respiratory Blend over lungs and place 2-3 drops in a diffuser. Apply Renewing Blend over the heart and on the back of the neck. Supporting the immune system is also an important part of grief recovery. Many of the above oils are chosen for both emotional properties and terpene content, which supports immune function.

Testimony/Story:

"I was going through intense grief with my husband's passing and unable to catch my breath to cope. I was exhausted, grief-stricken, and needing to rest. My friend brought over Comforting Blend and rubbed it over my heart and on the bottom of my feet. She also put Respiratory Blend in a diffuser in the room with me. Within minutes I was able to catch my breath and relax enough that I could stop crying and fall asleep. I used Comforting Blend every day over the next month and it was tremendously helpful. It made me feel like I was wrapped in loving arms." - Sandy G.

Protocol

» Apply 3 drops Melissa, 2 drops Marjoram, and 2 drops Geranium onto cotton-wick inhaler and inhale deeply multiple times per day (refresh oils often).[33] Or place 1 drop of each oil in palms and inhale deeply. Can be done every 1-2 hours if needed.

» Take 1-3 capsules of Restful Complex Softgels 30 min before bed or to help with napping during the day if unable to sleep restfully at night.[34]

» Apply 2 drops each of Rose, Frankincense, and Neroli to neck and massage into neck and shoulders with fractionated coconut oil 2-3 times daily (these oils may also be used in an aromatherapy inhaler).[35]

» Apply Comforting Blend or Centering Blend over heart or diffuse in room.

Suggested Duration:

Use protocol daily for the first 2-3 weeks following bereavement. Continue 1-3 methods above daily for 3 months.

Betrayal

Oils and Blends:

Bergamot, Black Pepper, Rose, Frankincense, Geranium, Lemon, Neroli, Marjoram, Melissa, Roman Chamomile, Cypress, Peppermint, Rosemary, Grapefruit, Turmeric, Wintergreen, Respiratory Blend, Centering Blend, Reassuring Blend, Enlightening Blend, Soothing Blend, Tension Blend

Supplements:

Restful Complex Softgels

Additional Support:

Try sprinkling 2 drops each of Frankincense, Roman Chamomile, and Lavender onto cotton-wick inhaler and inhale deeply multiple times per day (refresh oils often). Or place 1 drop of each oil in palms and inhale deeply. Apply Soothing Blend to neck and shoulders to release emotional tension. Add in Restful Complex Softgels before bedtime. Or try adding 3 drops Cypress to cotton-wick inhaler along with 3 drops Melissa, 2 drops Marjoram, and 2 drops Geranium. Diffuse 3 drops each of Frankincense, Lemon, and Cypress during the day. Apply 1 drop each Peppermint and Geranium over the heart and deeply inhale aroma for 5 breaths.

Testimony/Story:

"When my marriage ended I was left feeling so disheartened and betrayed. My best friend started coming over daily and just sitting with me while she diffused a mix of Grapefruit, Wild Orange, Lemon, and Bergamot while she would just let me talk. I noticed I always felt lighter after she left even though she never gave me any advice. She gifted me a bottle of Wintergreen and I would inhale it from the bottle and feel the heaviness lift from my heart. I began to regularly use these oils and started to feel whole again. They got me over the hurdle and I'm thankful." - Kayla

Protocol

» Alternate between Reassuring Blend and Respiratory blend, applying over the heart throughout the day.[36]

» Diffuse 2 drops each Grapefruit, Wild Orange, Lemon, and Bergamot to lighten mood.[37]

» Apply 3 drops Melissa, 2 drops Marjoram, and 2 drops Geranium onto cotton-wick inhaler and inhale deeply multiple times per day (refresh oils often). Or place 1 drop of each oil in palms and inhale deeply. Can be done every 1-2 hours if needed.[38]

» Apply 2 drops Centering Blend or 2 drops Enlightening Blend to back of neck or bottoms of feet.

» Inhale Wintergreen or Rosemary directly from their bottles, apply Tension Blend to neck.

» Take 1 drop of Turmeric oil internally in vegetable capsule twice daily with meals.

Suggested Duration:

Use as needed in situations of feeling betrayal. Use daily for 1 month if betrayal is fresh or has been held in body unprocessed for a long time. Continue using any methods that support moving beyond feelings of betrayal.

Bipolar Disorder (Manic)

Oils and Blends:

Frankincense, Copaiba, Blue Tansy, Lemon, Spearmint, Rose, Basil, Coriander, Tangerine, Spikenard, Ylang Ylang, Vetiver, Restful Blend, Reassuring Blend, Grounding Blend

Supplements:

Vitality Supplement Trio, Copaifera Softgels, Restful Blend Softgels

---

Additional Support:

Take Vitality Supplement Trio twice daily, the omega's support the brain. Apply Reassuring Blend down spine, back of neck throughout the day. Inhale Basil or Coriander straight from the bottle for 5 breaths. Apply Kid's Restful Blend on the bottom of feet throughout the day.

Protocol

» 2 drops Frankincense or Copaiba under the tongue 2x daily (or use 1-2 Copaifera Softgels 2x daily). [39]

» Apply Restful Blend over heart and Grounding Blend to feet.[40]

» Apply 3 drops Blue Tansy and Lemon onto cotton-wick inhaler and carry with you, inhaling deeply for 5 breaths multiple times per day (refresh oils often).[41] Or place 1 drop of each oil in palms and inhale from hands several times a day.

» Diffuse 2 drops Spearmint, 1 drop Ylang Ylang, 3 drops Tangerine during the day.[42]

» Take Restful Blend Softgels 30 minutes before bedtime and diffuse 2 drops Spikenard with 3 drops Vetiver next to bed (Or apply these oils to the bottoms of your feet).

Suggested Duration:

Use daily to support a healthy and even mood state. Use ongoing for support in a consistent manner.bereavement. Continue 1-3 methods above daily for 3 months.

Bipolar Disorder (Depressive)

Oils and Blends:

Frankincense, Copaiba, Bergamot, Lime, Melissa, Oregano, Peppermint, Rosemary, Inspiring Blend, Uplifting Blend, Encouraging Blend, Enlightening Blend, Comforting Blend

Supplements:

Vitality Supplement Trio, Copaifera Softgels

Additional Support:

Apply 1 drop each of Lime and Bergamot oils around navel. Take Vitality Supplement Trio twice daily. Apply Comforting Blend over heart and on the back of the neck, massage in thoroughly and take 5 deep breaths. Research shows that a property known as carvacrol in Oregano and Thyme essential oils may alleviate depression and promote feelings of well being. The Omega's in Vitality Trio will help with brain health and healing.

Protocol

» 2 drops Frankincense or Copaiba under the tongue twice daily (or use 1-2 Copaifera Softgels twice daily). You can also use both at the same time.[43]

» 1 drop of Melissa oil to thumb, then press to the roof of your mouth while holding for 15 seconds.[44]

» Diffuse Peppermint and Rosemary together in equal parts.[45]

» Diffuse 2-3 drops Enlightening Blend.

» Apply Inspiring Blend, Uplifting Blend, or Encouraging Blend over heart. Deeply inhale aroma for 5 breaths.

Suggested Duration:

Use daily to support a healthy and even mood state. Use ongoing for support in a consistent manner.bereavement. Continue 1-3 methods above daily for 3 months.

Bipolar Disorder (Mixed Episodes)

Oils and Blends:

Frankincense, Copaiba,Bergamot, Blue Tansy, Lemon, Grapefruit, Wild Orange, Spikenard, Ylang Ylang, Vetiver, Oregano, Kid's Grounding Blend

Supplements:

Vitality Supplement Trio, Copaifera Softgels, Restful Blend Softgels

---

Additional Support:

Take Vitality Supplement Trio twice daily for added brain support. Apply Kid's Grounding Blend over heart and on the back of the neck, then take 5 deep breaths. Take 1 drop Oregano daily in empty vegetable capsule (with food) 2x daily. Research shows that a property known as carvacrol in Oregano essential oil may alleviate depression.

Protocol

» 2 drops Frankincense or Copaiba under the tongue 2x daily (or use 1-2 Copaifera Softgels 2x daily).[46]

» Apply 3 drops Blue Tansy and Lemon onto cotton-wick inhaler and carry with you, inhaling deeply for 5 breaths multiple times per day (refresh oils often).[47] Or place 1 drop of each oil in palms and inhale from hands.

» Take Restful Blend Softgels 30 min before bedtime and diffuse 2 drops Spikenard with 3 drops Vetiver next to bed (you can also apply these oils to the bottoms of your feet).

» Diffuse 2 drops each of Grapefruit, Wild Orange, Lemon, and Bergamot when feeling irritable or depressed.[48]

Suggested Duration:

Use daily to support a healthy and even mood state. Use ongoing for support in a consistent manner.bereavement. Continue 1-3 methods above daily for 3 months.

Bitterness

Oils and Blends:

Birch, Lemon, Neroli, Lavender, Rosemary, Fennel, Cinnamon, Siberian Fir, Cedarwood, Renewing Blend, Comforting Blend, Captivating Blend, Tension Blend

---

Additional Support:

Try diffusing 2 drops each of Cedarwood and Siberian Fir. Inhale Birch directly from bottle. Apply Captivating Blend to palms and deeply inhale for 5 breaths. Or try the protocol for Resentment.

Protocol

» Apply Comforting Blend or Renewing Blend over heart.

» Apply 3 drops each of Lavender, Lemon, and Neroli onto cotton-wick inhaler and inhale deeply multiple times per day (refresh oils often). Or place 1 drop of each oil in palms and inhale deeply. Can be done every 1-2 hours if needed.

» Diffuse 1 drop each Cinnamon, Fennel, and Rosemary.

» Apply Tension Blend to neck and temples near hairline (avoiding eye area).

Suggested Duration:

Use as needed. Use daily if experiencing intense feelings of bitterness.

Body Dismorphia

Oils and Blends:

Douglas Fir, Siberian Fir, Arborvitae, Eucalyptus, Melissa, Basil, Jasmine, Magnolia, Spearmint, Anti-Aging Blend, Topical Blend, Balancing Blend, Renewing Blend, Comforting Blend, Kid's Courage Blend, Kid's Restful Blend, Kid's Grounding Blend

Supplements:

Fruit and Veggie Drink, Vitality Trio Supplement

Additional Support:

Try applying Comforting Blend or Renewing Blend over the heart. While in the shower, apply 1 drop each of Siberian Fir and Eucalyptus to tops of feet and massage while working oil up the feet, ankles, and calves. Use Kid's Courage Blend, Kid's Restful Blend, Kid's Grounding Blend as perfume on wrists. Also, look at protocols for Obsessive Compulsive Disorder or Depression.

Testimony/Story:

"I had gained a ton of weight and then lost some weight again, but no matter how much weight I lost I still saw a heavy man staring back at me in the mirror. In my mind, I heard my grade school classmates chanting and teasing me while I felt like I would never be thin enough to overcome how heavy I felt. I hated my body no matter what it looked like. I started applying Jasmine to my body in the shower daily and over the course of about 3 weeks my attitude toward my body began to shift. Now, 3 months later, I can say I look in the mirror and LIKE who I see. I never thought I'd be here. These oils are miracle workers." - Jason M.

Protocol

» Diffuse 2 drops each Arborvitae and Spearmint and deeply inhale for 5 breaths.

» Apply Balancing Blend to abdomen and bottoms of feet and apply Anti-Aging Blend over the heart.

» Sprinkle 2 drops each of Melissa, Douglas Fir, and Basil onto cotton-wick inhaler and inhale deeply multiple times per day (refresh oils often).[49] Or place 1 drop of each oil in palms and inhale deeply.

» While showering, apply Jasmine to wet skin over heart and abdomen and thoroughly massage into skin.[50]

» Apply Magnolia to wrists to use as perfume and inhale aroma deeply for 4-5 breaths.

» Take 1 scoop Fruit and Veggie Drink in the morning, then the Vitality Supplement Trio twice daily to promote a healthy physical body.

» Use Topical Blend and Anti-Aging Blend to soothe blemishes and skin imperfections that cause self-doubt.

Suggested Duration:

Use daily for ongoing support or whenever feelings of body dysmorphia come up. Use any of the protocols that feel helpful to create an ongoing support of body positivity.

Broken Hearted

Oils and Blends:

Cinnamon, Melissa, Marjoram, Rose, Frankincense, Lemon, Geranium, Neroli, Cypress, Respiratory Blend, Comforting Blend, Renewing Blend, Centering Blend, Anti-Aging Blend, Inspiring Blend, Gathering Blend, Holiday Peaceful Blend

Supplements:

Restful Complex Softgels

Additional Support:

Try diffusing Holiday Peaceful Blend. Add 3 drops Cypress to cotton-wick inhaler along with 3 drops Melissa, 2 drops Marjoram, and 2 drops Geranium. Diffuse 3 drops each of Frankincense, Lemon, and Cypress during the day. If experiencing "heaviness" over chest, apply 2-3 drops Respiratory Blend over lungs and place 2-3 drops in a diffuser. Apply Renewing Blend over the heart and on the back of the neck. Apply Anti-Aging Blend over heart and back of neck. Another important part of grief recovery is supporting a healthy immune system. Many of the above oils are chosen for both emotional properties and terpene content, which supports immune function.

Testimony/Story:

"A friend lost her husband suddenly and was overcome with grief. It was weeks and she still hadn't slept more than just a few hours each night. I went over to her home and did a light touch massage on her. I layered Rose, Frankincense and Neroli down her spine. She called me the next day and said it was the first time that she was able to sleep since the loss. I repeated the massage several more times with similar results. It really helped her through a time of loss." -Jenna B.

Protocol

» Apply 3 drops Melissa, 2 drops Marjoram, and 2 drops Geranium onto cotton-wick inhaler and inhale deeply multiple times per day (refresh oils often).[51] Or place 1 drop of each oil in palms and inhale deeply. Can be done every 1-2 hours if needed.

» Take 1-3 capsules of Restful Complex Softgels 30 min before bed or to help with napping during the day if unable to sleep restfully at night.

» Apply 2 drops each of Rose, Frankincense, and Neroli to neck and massage into neck and shoulders with fractionated coconut oil 2-3 times daily (these oils may also be used in an aromatherapy inhaler).[52]

» Apply Comforting Blend, Gathering Blend, or Centering Blend over heart or diffuse in room.

» Diffuse 2 drops Cinnamon or apply Inspiring Blend over heart to inspire new possibilities and vigor for life.[53]

Suggested Duration:

Use daily, consistently, in an ongoing manner until feelings subside.

Bulimia

Oils and Blends:

Bergamot, Ylang Ylang, Geranium, Clary Sage, Fennel, Eucalyptus, Frankincense, Ginger, Jasmine, Lemon, Rosemary, Spearmint, Metabolic Blend, Digestive Blend, Renewing Blend, Invigorating Blend

Supplements:

Fruit and Veggie Drink

Additional Support:

Try sprinkling 3 drops each of Clary Sage and Eucalyptus onto cotton-wick inhaler and inhale deeply multiple times per day (refresh oils often). Or place 1 drop of each oil in palms and inhale deeply. Apply Jasmine over heart. Diffuse 3 drops Lemon, 2 drops Rosemary, 2 drops Spearmint. Take 1 scoop of Fruit and Veggie drink in the morning.

Protocol

» Diffuse 3 drops Bergamot, 2 drops Ylang Ylang, and 2 drops Geranium to support love and appreciation of self.[54]

» Apply Renewing Blend over heart and deeply inhale for 5 breaths.

» Inhale Fennel directly from the bottle or apply 1 drop Fennel to tongue to soothe intense cravings.[55]

» Drink 12 oz of water mixed with 2 drops Metabolic Blend to inhibit binging episodes and support healthy blood sugar levels.

» Apply 2 drops Digestive Blend around naval or drink 1 drop in 4 oz of water to reduce nausea, feelings of discomfort in the stomach, or purging behaviors.

» Diffuse 3 drops each of Frankincense and Ginger or Invigorating Blend to uplift mood.[56]

Suggested Duration:

Use daily or as needed to ward off unwanted food habits and behaviors. Continue to use daily to support mental peace around food.

Codependency

Oils and Blends:

Basil, Lavender, Cinnamon, Cypress, Bergamot, Frankincense, Myrrh, Cardamom, Marjoram, Roman Chamomile, Douglas Fir, Siberian Fir, Tea Tree, Grapefruit, Clove Bud, Lemongrass, Wintergreen, Yarrow|Pom, Inspiring Blend, Kid's Courage Blend, Reassuring Blend, Comforting Blend, Soothing Blend, Tension Blend, Protective Blend

Additional Support:

Try sprinkling 2 drops Clove Bud, 6 drops Grapefruit, 2 drops Roman Chamomile to cotton-wick inhaler and inhale deeply multiple times per day (refresh oils often) If you don't have inhaler put 1 drop of each oil in a diffuser. Diffuse regularly. This blend may be helpful with establishing general boundaries with confidence, grace, and calmness. Inhale Wintergreen oil directly from the bottle. Apply Soothing Blend to neck and shoulders to release emotional tension. Apply Tension Blend to bottoms of feet. Diffuse Protective Blend. Apply Yarrow|Pom to palms and deeply inhale aroma.

Testimony/Story:

"I used to feel very needy and dependent on my parents even as an adult. I wanted their approval and involvement in every area of my life--until it became too stressful for our relationship. I began applying Reassuring Blend over my heart daily and diffusing 1 drop each of Cypress, Bergamot, Douglas Fir, and affirming "I deeply love and accept myself for all my needs." Over time I began to feel more loving and accepting towards myself, feeling capable on my own, and needing their approval and direction less and less." - Cindy L.

Protocol

» Apply Kid's Courage Blend, Reassuring Blend, or Comforting blend over the heart.

» Apply 2 drops Basil, 3 drops Lavender, and 3 drops Lime to diffuser and deeply inhale while sitting next to it. Or apply 1 drop of each to palms of hands and deeply inhale for 5 deep breaths. This blend may help with speaking your needs confidently and advocating for self.

» Diffuse 1 drop each of Cinnamon, Tea Tree, Cardamom, Lemongrass. This blend may be helpful in breaking free from codependent bonds with close friends and romantic partners.

» Diffuse 1 drop each of Cypress, Bergamot, Douglas Fir or Siberian Fir. This blend may be helpful in breaking free from codependent behavior in general.

» Apply 2 drops each of Myrrh, Marjoram, Frankincense to cotton-wick inhaler and inhale deeply multiple times per day (refresh oils often). Or place 1 drop of each oil in palms and inhale deeply. Can be done every 1-2 hours if needed. This blend may be helpful in breaking free from codependent bonds with parents and immediate family members.

Suggested Duration:

Use daily for 2-3 months. Use these protocols consistently until relationship dynamics and patterns begin to shift in the areas of your life you want to see change.

Conduct Disorder

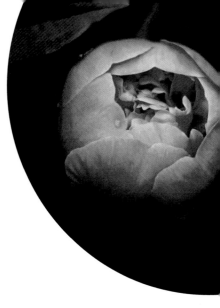

Oils and Blends:

Copaiba, Grapefruit, Wild Orange, Lemon, Bergamot, Frankincense, Peppermint, Melissa, Vetiver, Focus Blend, Kid's Focus Blend, Reassuring Blend, Restful Blend, Kid's Restful Blend

Supplements:

Copaifera Softgels

Additional Support:

Try adding 1-2 Copaifera Softgels twice daily. Diffuse 6-7 drops of Frankincense and apply oil down spine and back of neck. For children over 12 years old put 1 drop of Melissa oil on thumb and press thumb to the roof of the mouth and hold for 15 seconds. Apply 2 drops Vetiver over heart or diffuse 3 drops each of Vetiver and Frankincense.

Testimony/Story:

"I had a high school student in my classroom with this diagnosis who was constantly giving every teacher a hard time everyday. Out of desperation we began diffusing Reassuring Blend in a diffuser nearby his desk and noticed that his outbursts started becoming less frequent and less intense. Then we made aromatherapy inhalers as a craft project one day, and I gave him a selection of oils to choose from, he picked all citrus oils for his. As a class we began using the inhalers as a routine throughout the day when transitioning between subjects/activities. We instructed kids to use them on their own when they felt overwhelmed and I was amazed at how this kid began to soften and relax when he used his inhaler. I am a believer!" - Jaime E.

Protocol

» Apply Reassuring Blend, Restful Blend, or Kid's Restful Blend over heart. May choose to cycle through these three oils applied throughout the day every couple of hours. Take 6 deep breaths and deeply inhale aroma each time they are applied.

» Diffuse 2 drops each of Grapefruit, Wild Orange, Lemon, and Bergamot to promote calm, uplifting environment.[57]

» Sprinkle 4 drops Frankincense, 3 drops Wild Orange, and 2 drops Peppermint onto cotton-wick inhaler and inhale deeply multiple times per day (refresh oils often). Or place 1 drop of each oil in palms and inhale deeply.

» Apply Focus Blend or Kid's Focus Blend to back of neck before performing tasks, schoolwork, or anything that requires specific focus and attention.

Suggested Duration:

Use daily in an ongoing manner as a preventative measure to help keep defiance and oppositional behavior at bay. Choose one or two above protocols as interventions to use when defiant behavior occurs.

Confusion

Oils and Blends:

Peppermint, Rosemary, Basil, Arborvitae, Frankincense, Lavender, Lemon, Rose, Eucalyptus, Melissa, Holiday Peaceful Blend, Focus Blend, Kid's Focus Blend

Supplements:

Children's Omega, Essential Oil + Omega Complex

Additional Support:

Try diffusing Holiday Peaceful Blend. Add 3 drops Arborvitae, 2 drops Rosemary, 2 drops Peppermint to diffuser. Add in Children's Omega's twice a day or the Essential Oil + Omega Complex twice daily. Also see protocol for Alzheimers.

Testimony/Story:

"My 7th grade daughter used to come home from school everyday with math homework and just say, "I don't know! My teacher is confusing! I don't get it!" and she didn't want to work on it together or have a tutor for math. Together we came up with a blend that we called her 'Confusion Clearing Super Elixir' made from Peppermint, Basil, and Rosemary oils and she was willing to try inhaling it before meeting with a math tutor. During tutoring she began to understand more math and when she felt confused, she would inhale the blend we made her. Soon, she was beginning to grow in confidence and math skills in tutoring and wanted to take her blend to school to try in class. I believe using this blend in both tutoring and class gave her the confidence to believe she could figure out anything she was confused by. She passed math with a B+!" - Sara W.

Protocol

» Diffuse 2 drops each of Peppermint, Rosemary, and Basil essential oils.[58]

» Apply 3 drops Lemon, 2 drops Rose, and 3 drops Eucalyptus to cotton-wick inhaler and inhale deeply multiple times per day (refresh oils often). Or place 1 drop of each oil in palms and inhale deeply. Can be done every 1-2 hours if needed.

» Apply Focus blend or Kid's Focus Blend to back of neck and rub in thoroughly at base of head at hairline.

» Apply 3 drops Frankincense, 2 drops Lavender, and 2 drops Melissa to cotton-wick inhaler and inhale deeply multiple times per day (refresh oils often).[59] Or place 1 drop of each oil in palms and inhale deeply. Can be done every 1-2 hours if needed.

Suggested Duration:

Use as needed in moments of confusion. Use daily if an ongoing lack of clarity and confusion is persistent or if struggling with confusion due to brain degeneration or disease.

Controlling

Oils and Blends:

Blue Tansy, Cardamom, Sandalwood, Vetiver, Frankincense, Lemon, Marjoram, Myrrh, Grapefruit, Roman Chamomile, Lavender, Restful Blend, Reassuring Blend, Grounding Blend, Cleansing Blend

Additional Support:

Try applying Restful Blend to back of neck and bottoms of the feet. Apply Reassuring Blend over heart. Diffuse Cleaning Blend to purify the environment energetically.

Protocol

» Apply Grounding Blend to bottoms of feet.

» Apply Respiratory Blend over heart and take 4-5 deep breaths.

» Diffuse 3 drops each of Lemon, Marjoram, and Lavender to relax and uplift mood.[60]

» Apply 2 drops Blue Tansy, 2 drops Vetiver, and 3 drops Grapefruit to cotton-wick inhaler and inhale for 5 breaths 3-4 times per day (refresh with oils every 5 days).

» Put 1 drop of each oil in a diffuser: Clove Bud, Grapefruit,Roman Chamomile. Diffuse regularly. This blend may be helpful with trusting others to navigate their own life and to curb the need to control outcomes less.

Suggested Duration:

Use daily as needed to stop the need to control situations and interject yourself in areas that are no longer your responsibility.

Critical

Oils and Blends:

Birch, Grapefruit, Wild Orange, Lemon, Bergamot, Frankincense, Rosemary, Blue Tansy, Lemon, Metabolic Blend, Inspiring Blend, Uplifting Blend, Invigorating Blend, Joyful Blend, Comforting Blend, Renewing Blend, Restful Blend, Holiday Peaceful Blend

Supplements:

Copaifera Softgels

Additional Support:

Try applying Comforting Blend and Renewing Blend over heart. Inhale Birch directly from bottle. Diffuse Uplifting Blend. Diffuse 2 drops Rosemary and 3 drops Frankincense. Drink 8oz of water with 1 drop Metabolic Blend in it.

Protocol

» Apply Restful Blend over heart and diffuse Joyful Blend.

» Diffuse 2 drops each Grapefruit, Wild Orange, Lemon, and Bergamot.[61]

» Place 1 drop of each, Blue Tansy and Lemon in palms and inhale deeply. Can be done every 1-2 hours as needed.

» Diffuse Holiday Peaceful Blend and deeply inhale for 5 breaths.

Suggested Duration:

Use as needed when feelings of critique come to the surface.

Debilitated

Oils and Blends:

Cypress, Eucalyptus, Frankincense, Coriander, Patchouli, Peppermint, Juniper Berry, Clary Sage, Bergamot, Wild Orange, Ginger, Cedarwood, Thyme, Lemongrass, Rosemary, Yarrow|Pom, Uplifting Blend, Comforting Blend, Holiday Joyful Blend

Supplements:

Energy & Stamina Complex, Cellular Complex Softgels

Additional Support:

Try exchanging Ginger, Thyme, Coriander, or Cedarwood for Juniper Berry in the above inhaler protocol. Also consider adding 1-2 drops Lemongrass to diffuser blend above with 2 drops each of Wild Orange, Bergamot, and Rosemary. Take 1-2 Energy & Stamina Complex once in the morning to promote energy and movement to get the body going. Take 2 Cellular Complex Softgels twice daily for cellular and brain support. Put 1 drop of Peppermint oil into 12 oz of water and drink to enhance alertness and energy. Diffuse Holiday Joyful Blend.

Testimony/Story:

"Whenever I am feeling emotionally overwhelmed and totally debilitated, I reach for my Energy & Stamina Complex, my Wild Orange, Bergamot, and Rosemary essential oils. I use them in the morning, and sometimes mid-day if I am in a slump and just can't seem to find the motivation for what to do next. I find that these will help me snap back into action. I sit next to my diffuser and take long, deep inhales of the vapor. With each breath I feel my energy begin to come back to me while I regain my will to get tasks done."
- Kaitie K.

Protocol

» Diffuse 2 drops each Wild Orange, Bergamot, and Rosemary to uplift, enliven, and support self-confidence in actions.[62]

» Alternate between applying Comforting Blend and Uplifting Blend over the heart throughout the day.

» Apply 2 drops each of Cypress, Eucalyptus, Frankincense, and Juniper Berry onto cotton-wick inhaler (refresh inhaler with new oils every 3-7 days).[63] If you don't have inhaler place 1 drop each in palms of hands and deeply inhale for 5 breaths. Alternatively, this blend works well in a diffuser.

» Apply 1 drop Patchouli to cotton-wick inhaler and inhale deeply multiple times per day (refresh oils often) Or place 1 drop of oil in palms and inhale deeply. Can be done every 1-2 hours if needed.

» Apply Yarrow|Pom to palms and deeply inhale aroma.[64]

Suggested Duration:

Use protocol consecutively for two weeks. Continue using any of the above methods that feel supportive to you as needed ongoing forward.

Delusions

Oils and Blends:

Clove Bud, Copaiba, Eucalyptus, Frankincense, Grapefruit, Helichrysum, Lavender, Lemon, Melissa, Peppermint, Roman Chamomile, Rose, Rosemary, Basil, Spearmint, Spikenard, Vetiver, Wild Orange, Ylang Ylang, Steadying Blend, Restful Blend, Reassuring Blend

Supplements:

Copaifera Softgels

Additional Support:

Try sprinkling 2 drops Clove Bud, 6 drops Grapefruit, 2 drops Roman Chamomile to cotton-wick inhaler and inhale deeply multiple times per day (refresh oils often). Or put 1 drop of each oil in a diffuser. Diffuse regularly. Inhale Basil directly from the bottle. Or sprinkle 1 drop Geranium, 1 drop Melissa, 1 drop Ylang Ylang, and 3 drops Frankincense onto cotton-wick inhaler and inhale deeply multiple times per day (refresh oils often). Or place 1 drop of each oil in palms and inhale deeply. Can be done every 1-2 hours if needed.

Testimony/Story:

"Restful Blend has been a game changer for my uncle who suffers from delusions. Just diffusing it or applying it to him topically begins to snap him out of it! Thank God for oils!"
 - Cate C.

Protocol

» Diffuse Steadying Blend or Restful Blend.[65]

» Take 2 Copaifera Softgels twice daily.

» Apply 3 drops Vetiver or Reassuring Blend over heart and deeply inhale for 5-6 breaths.[66]

» Diffuse 2 drops each of Spearmint, Wild Orange, and Peppermint.

» Apply 3 drops Lemon, 2 drops Rose, and 3 drops Eucalyptus to cotton-wick inhaler and inhale deeply multiple times per day (refresh oils often).[67] Or place 1 drop of each oil in palms and inhale deeply. Can be done every 1-2 hours if needed.

» Sprinkle 2 drops each of Ylang Ylang, Spikenard, and Helichrysum onto cotton-wick inhaler and inhale deeply multiple times per day (refresh oils often).[68] Or place 1 drop of each oil in hands and inhale deeply.

» Put 1 drop of Melissa oil to thumb and press it to the roof of the mouth, holding for 15 seconds.[69]

Suggested Duration:

Use daily as a preventative measure in an ongoing basis. Use as needed in moments of delusion.

Depersonalization

Oils and Blends:

Clary Sage, Rosemary, Thyme, Ylang Ylang, Wild Orange, Magnolia, Peppermint, Grounding Blend, Joyful Blend, Invigorating Blend, Encouraging Blend, Renewing Blend

Additional Support:

Try adding Encouraging Blend and Renewing Blend over the heart. Diffuse 3 drops Thyme, 4 drops Wild Orange, 2 drops Ylang Ylang.

Testimony/Story:

"I used to get scared because I would feel like I wasn't real, my room wasn't real and I would have fears that I would open my door and the world would be gone. I would feel disconnected from every other person and form of life on the earth. When I started diffusing Joyful Blend and Encouraging Blend together, I would feel immediately like I was coming back into my body and like everything was going to be okay again. I always keep Peppermint on my person just in case I need a quick zap to my mind to bring me back in my daily life." - Breanne C.

Protocol

» Diffuse a mix of 3 drops each of Joyful Blend and Invigorating Blend.

» Rub 3-4 drops Grounding Blend on bottom of each foot.

» Apply 3 drops each of Peppermint, Rosemary, Clary Sage onto cotton-wick inhaler and inhale deeply multiple times per day (refresh oils often). Or place 1 drop of each oil in palms and inhale deeply. Can be done every 1-2 hours if needed.

» Inhale Magnolia from the bottle or apply it to wrists/neck as perfume.

Suggested Duration:

Use during episodes of depersonalization to pull person out of state of being. Use 1-2 protocols daily as a preventative or use daily for 3 months if feelings of disconnect are chronic.

Depression

Oils and Blends:

Frankincense, Copaiba, Lime, Bergamot, Peppermint, Rosemary, Melissa, Blue Tansy, Lemon, Inspiring Blend, Uplifting Blend, Encouraging Blend, Invigorating Blend, Joyful Blend, Enlightening Blend, Holiday Peaceful Blend

Supplements:

Vitality Supplement Trio, Polyphenol Complex, Copaifera Softgels

Additional Support:

If you're not yet seeing the results you'd like to see, try adding 1 drop of Melissa oil to thumb and pressing to the roof of your mouth and holding for 15 seconds. Diffuse Citrus Bliss or Elevation, or a combination of the two oils. Take 2 drops each of Frankincense and Copaiba together internally. Research also shows that depression can be caused by inflammation in the brain, adding in the Polyphenol Complex twice daily may help reduce inflammation and, therefore, depression as well.

Testimony/Story:

"I thought I had tried everything--nothing was helping me with my feelings of listlessness and apathy. I felt in a fog. I started taking the Vitality Trio daily and then added in Frankincense and Copaiba under my tongue, along with diffusing Peppermint, Rosemary, and the Invigorating Blend in my home and office and I swear to you the fog began to lift! I can actually feel hopeful and light now, whereas before all I could see was darkness." - Jenna K.

Protocol

» 2 drops Frankincense or Copaiba under the tongue twice daily (or use Copaifera Softgels).

» Diffuse Peppermint and Rosemary together in equal parts.[70]

» Apply 3 drops each of Blue Tansy and Lemon onto cotton-wick inhaler and inhale deeply multiple times per day (refresh oils often).[71] Or place 1 drop of each oil in palms and inhale deeply. Can be done every 1-2 hours if needed.

» Diffuse 2-3 drops of Enlightening Blend or Holiday Peaceful Blend.

» Apply 1 drop each of Lime and Bergamot oils around navel. Do not expose skin with Bergamot or Lime to direct sunlight for 24 hours.

» Apply Inspiring Blend, Uplifting Blend, or Encouraging Blend over your heart. Deeply inhale aroma for 5 breaths.

» Take Vitality Supplement Trio twice daily.

Suggested Duration:

Use for 3-4 months minimum. Continue 1-3 of the above methods daily for as long as needed.

Despair

Oils and Blends:

Melissa, Marjoram, Rose, Frankincense, Lemon, Geranium, Neroli, Cypress, Respiratory Blend, Comforting Blend, Renewing Blend, Centering Blend, Patchouli, Eucalyptus, Wild Orange

---

Additional Support:

Try diffusing 3 drops each of Frankincense, Lemon, and Cypress during the day. If experiencing "heaviness" over chest, apply 2-3 drops Respiratory Blend over lungs and place 2-3 drops in a diffuser. Put 1 drop of Peppermint oil in 12 oz of water and drink to enhance alertness and energy. Apply 1 drop Patchouli to cotton-wick inhaler and inhale deeply multiple times per day (refresh with new oil every 3-7 days) Or place 1 drop of oil in palms and inhale deeply. Can be done every 1-2 hours if needed. Apply Centering Blend over heart.

Protocol

» Diffuse 2 drops each Wild Orange, Bergamot, & Rosemary.[72]

» Alternate applying the Comforting Blend and the Renewing Blend over the heart throughout the day.

» Apply 2 drops each of Rose, Frankincense, and Neroli to back of neck and massage into neck and shoulders with fractionated coconut oil 2-3 times daily (these oils may also be used in an aromatherapy inhaler).[73]

» Apply 3 drops Melissa, 2 drops Marjoram, and 2 drops Geranium onto cotton-wick inhaler and inhale deeply multiple times per day (refresh oils often).[74] Or place 1 drop of each oil in palms and inhale deeply. Can be done every 1-2 hours if needed.

» Diffuse 2 drops each Eucalyptus and Peppermint.[75]

Suggested Duration:

Use protocol for 1 month consecutively. Continue using any protocols that feel supportive to you as needed.

Difficulty with Transitions

Oils and Blends:

Lavender, Frankincense, Rosemary, Peppermint, Lemon, Wild Orange, Reassuring Blend, Restful Blend, Focus Blend, Kid's Focus Blend

Supplements:

Fruit and Veggie Drink, Vitality Supplement Trip, Children's Omegas, Children's Chewable

---

Additional Support:

Try adding in the Vitality Supplement Trio twice a day for adults. For kids, add in the Children's Chewables and Children's Omega-3 daily. Both children and adults will benefit from Fruit and Veggie Drink in the morning. Diffuse Lemon, Wild Orange, and Peppermint to uplift and energize the mind.

Protocol

» Diffuse 3 drops each of Lavender and Frankincense prior to times of transition.

» Apply Focus Blend, Kid's Focus Blend to back of the neck, massaging in thoroughly at base of hairline into the brain stem. May also apply down spine for extra boost.

» Apply Reassuring Blend over heart.

» Sprinkle 2 drops each of Frankincense, Rosemary, and Peppermint onto cotton-wick inhaler and inhale deeply multiple times per day (refresh oils often). Or place 1 drop of each oil in palms and inhale deeply.

Suggested Duration:

Use daily prior to transitions to help create relaxed and resilient atmosphere. Continue to use in ongoing manner for daily support.

Disconnected

Oils and Blends:

Basil, Rosemary, Thyme, Jasmine, Ylang Ylang, Wild Orange, Magnolia, Mānuka, Peppermint, Grounding Blend, Gathering Blend, Joyful Blend, Invigorating Blend, Encouraging Blend, Renewing Blend, Uplifting Blend, Focus Blend, Kid's Focus Blend

---

Additional Support:

Try adding Encouraging Blend and Renewing Blend over the heart. Diffuse 4-5 drps Gathering Blend. Diffuse 3 drops Thyme, 4 drops Wild Orange, and 2 drops Ylang Ylang. Apply Mānuka to the wrists.

Protocol

» Diffuse a mix of 3 drops each of Joyful Blend and Invigorating Blend.

» Rub 3-4 drops of Grounding Blend on bottom of each foot.

» Apply Inspiring Blend or Uplifting Blend over heart.

» Apply 3 drops each of Peppermint, Rosemary, Basil onto cotton-wick inhaler and inhale deeply multiple times per day (refresh oils often). Or place 1 drop of each oil in palms and inhale deeply. Can be done every 1-2 hours if needed.

» For Women: Inhale Magnolia from the bottle or apply it to wrists/neck as perfume.

» For Men: Inhale InTune from the bottle or apply it to wrists/neck as cologne.

» For Kids: Inhale Kid's Focus Blend from bottle or apply to back of neck and chest.

Suggested Duration:

Use when feeling disconnected from life, people, purpose, or reality. Use 1-2 protocols daily as preventative or use daily for 3 months if feelings of disconnectedness are chronic. See also protocol for Depersonalization.

Discouraged

Oils and Blends:

Cypress, Douglas Fir, Lemongrass, Ginger, Jasmine, Juniper Berry, Thyme, Lime, Rosemary, Geranium, Sandalwood, Comforting Blend, Renewing Blend, Inspiring Blend, Captivating Blend

Supplements:

Copaifera Softgels

Additional Support:

Try adding Copaifera Softgels twice daily. Diffuse 1 drop Geranium, 2 drops Douglas Fir, 2 drops Thyme. Apply Inspiring Blend over the heart. Apply Captivating Blend to the wrists.

Testimony/Story:

"I work in sales and my monthly income is determined by the commissions I make that month. Whenever it's getting towards the end of my quota period and I am feeling a bit discouraged about my potential paycheck, I slather Inspiring Blend over my heart and inhale my aromatherapy inhaler between sales conversations. It never fails to give me the boost I need..."- Gena S.

Protocol

» Apply 3 drops each of Cypress, Lime, Sandalwood, and Lemongrass to cotton-wick inhaler and inhale deeply multiple times per day (refresh oils often).

» Apply Comforting Blend & Renewing Blend over the heart.

» Diffuse 2 drops each of Ginger, Juniper Berry, and Rosemary.

Suggested Duration:

Use daily for 2 months if feelings are chronic or use as needed during moments of intense feelings of discouragement.

Distrusting

Oils and Blends:

Lavender, Douglas Fir, Siberian Fir, Vetiver, Lemon, Grapefruit, Wild Orange, Grounding Blend, Reassuring Blend, Kid's Courage Blend, Restful Blend, Gathering Blend, Captivating Blend

---

Additional Support:

Try diffusing Restful Blend or Gathering Blend Apply Captivating Blend to the wrists.

Testimony/Story:

"After going through a really rough season of my life I was finding it hard to open up and trust people again. I had been badly burned and wanted to just rely on myself and never open up to anyone again. I knew about essential oils, so I started to use Lavender, Douglas Fir, and Wild Orange in my diffuser daily for about a month. I slowly began to feel safe again and comfortable reaching out to people, being able to rely on them again for friendship and support. It wasn't easy, but the essential oils definitely opened me up to new possibilities and made me feel more relaxed and willing to try new things instead of staying withdrawn to protect myself. I highly recommend that blend!" - Savannah B.

Protocol

» Apply Grounding Blend or Reassuring Blend to heart and inhale deeply.

» Diffuse 2-3 drops each of Lavender, Douglas Fir, and Wild Orange.

» Place 1 drop of each oil, Vetiver, Grapefruit, Siberian Fir Place in palms and inhale deeply. Can be done every 1-2 hours if needed.

Suggested Duration:

Use daily as needed to aid with feelings of distrust or unease.

Envy

Oils and Blends:

Wild Orange, Geranium, Ylang Ylang, Basil, Pink Pepper, Eucalyptus, Grapefruit, Juniper Berry, Roman Chamomile, Lavender, Bergamot, Lemon, Frankincense, Inspiring Blend, Uplifting Blend, Encouraging Blend, Steadying Blend

---

Additional Support:

Try applying Uplifting Blend or Encouraging Blend over the heart. Diffuse 4 drops Eucalyptus and deeply inhale aroma. Diffuse 2 drops Basil, 3 drops Lavender, and 2 drops Pink Pepper to calm the nervous system and enhance self worth.

Testimony/Story:

"I hate to admit this but in today's age of social media I find myself feeling envious and like my life is lacking all the time due to looking at my friends and strangers lives online. Whenever I feel incredibly envious ... I diffuse Ylang Ylang, Roman Chamomile, and Geranium in my diffuser and rub Inspiring Blend over my heart. It really helps to take the edge off and will snap me back to reality and being grateful for what I have." - Meaghan R.

Protocol

» Apply Inspiring Blend over the heart and take 5 deep breaths.

» Diffuse Steadying Blend and deeply inhale aroma.

» Sprinkle 2 drops each of Ylang Ylang, Roman Chamomile, and Geranium onto cotton-wick inhaler and inhale deeply multiple times per day (refresh oils often). Or place 1 drop of each oil in palms and inhale deeply.

» Diffuse 2 drops each Grapefruit, Wild Orange, Lemon, and Bergamot when feeling envious.[76]

Suggested Duration:

Use daily while experiencing feelings of envy. Continue to use as needed until feelings dissipate.

Embarrassed

Oils and Blends:

Bergamot, Copaiba, Ylang Ylang, Wild Orange, Black Pepper, Peppermint, Comforting Blend, Grounding Blend, Renewing Blend, Reassuring Blend, Respiratory Blend, Inspiring Blend, Joyful Blend, Invigorating Blend

Supplements:

Copaifera Softgels

Additional Support:

Try inhaling Black Pepper directly from the bottle for 5 deep breaths. Apply Grounding Blend to back of neck and bottoms of the feet. Diffuse Respiratory Blend. Mix 1 drop Peppermint with at least 12 oz water and drink. Take 1-2 Copaifera Softgels twice daily.

Protocol

» Apply Comforting Blend and Renewing Blend over the heart and take 4-5 deep breaths.

» Diffuse Reassuring Blend and deeply inhale aroma.

» Sprinkle 2 drops Bergamot, 1 drop Ylang Ylang, and 3 drops Wild Orange onto cotton-wick inhaler and inhale deeply multiple times per day (refresh oils often). Or place 1 drop of each oil in palms and inhale deeply.

» Apply Inspiring Blend over the heart.

» Diffuse 3 drops each of Joyful Blend and Invigorating Blend.

Suggested Duration:

Use for 1 week minimum. Use ongoing as needed for support or before confronting embarrassing situation.

Emptiness

Oils and Blends:

Bergamot, Lemon, Grapefruit, Geranium, Rose, Wild Orange, Frankincense, Ylang Ylang, Douglas Fir, Siberian Fir, Grounding Blend, Comforting Blend, Renewing Blend, Holiday Joyful Blend, Captivating Blend

---

Additional Support:

Try placing 1 drop each of Geranium and Ylang Ylang over the heart. Apply Captivating Blend on the wrists. Diffuse either Comforting Blend or Renewing Blend. Diffuse Holiday Joyful Blend. Bring Grapefruit into the shower with you and drop a few drops onto the side of the shower to let it diffuse while you shower. Also consider the "hot/cold" showers mentioned in the foundational supports in the intro section.

Protocol

» Diffuse 2 drops each Grapefruit, Wild Orange, Lemon, and Bergamot.[77]

» Apply Rose oil over the heart and deeply inhale for 5 breaths.

» Apply Grounding Blend on feet.

» Sprinkle 2 drops each of Frankincense, Douglas Fir, and Siberian Fir onto cotton-wick inhaler and inhale deeply multiple times per day (refresh oils often). Or place 1 drop of each oil in palms and inhale deeply.

Suggested Duration:

Use daily for a week at minimum. Use ongoing as needed to support emotions.

Fear

Oils and Blends:

Ylang Ylang, Copaiba, Lavender, Lemon, Melissa, Basil, Marjoram, Juniper Berry, Geranium, Vetiver, Rose, Cypress, Clary Sage, Wild Orange, Tea Tree, Holiday Joyful Blend, Restful Blend, Grounding Blend, Kid's Grounding Blend, Kid's Courage Blend, Kid's Restful Blend

Supplements:

Copaifera Softgel, Digestive Enzymes, Probiotic Complex, Restful Complex Softgels

Additional Support:

Try applying 1 drop each of Basil, Marjoram, Vetiver to bottoms of feet. Take Digestive Enzymes with every meal to settle fearful stomach and Probiotic Complex twice daily. Take Restful Complex Softgels before bed. Diffuse Clary Sage, Tea Tree, Wild Orange and Holiday Joyful Blend to uplift the mind and heart.

Protocol

» Apple 1 drop each of Cypress, Rose, and Juniper Berry to shoulders and massage in with fractionated coconut oil.[78]

» Diffuse 2 drops Copaiba, 1 drop Lavender, 2 drops Lemon or apply one drop of each to hands and rub around the navel.

» Place 1 drop of each oil, Geranium, Melissa, Ylang Ylang, Frankincense in palms and inhale every 1-2 hours as needed.

» Apply Grounding Blend & Restful Blend over heart and back of neck.

» For Kids: Apply Kid's Grounding Blend and Kid's Restful Blend over heart and down the spine. Diffuse 3-5 drops Juniper Berry next to bed to aid with night terrors.

Suggested Duration:

Use for 1 month. Continue to use as needed for ongoing support or in acute moments of fear.

Focus

Oils and Blends:

Rosemary, Basil, Black Pepper, Peppermint, Lemon, Grapefruit, Frankincense, Geranium, Cardamom, Focus Blend, Kid's Focus Blend

Supplements:

Energy & Stamina Complex, Fruit and Veggie Drink

Additional Support:

Try adding in Fruit and Veggie Drink in the morning for both kids and adults. For adults struggling with focus, also use the Energy & Stamina Complex once daily. Diffuse 2 drops each Peppermint, Rosemary, and Basil essential oils.

Protocol

» Apply Focus Blend or Kid's Focus Blend to back of neck, massaging thoroughly at base of hairline into the brain stem.

» Diffuse 2 drops Peppermint, 2 drops Rosemary, 3 drops Grapefruit in morning or during peak hours of needed focus and productivity.[79]

» Sprinkle 2 drops each of Rosemary, Lemon, and Black Pepper onto cotton-wick inhaler and inhale deeply multiple times per day (refresh oils often).[80] Or place 1 drop of each oil in palms and inhale deeply.

» Inhale Basil directly from the bottle.[81]

Suggested Duration:

Use daily ongoing as needed. These protocols are wonderfully supportive and can be used ongoing for as long as needed.

Frustrated

Oils and Blends:

Bergamot, Lemon, Grapefruit, Wild Orange, Peppermint, Blue Tansy, Vetiver, Renewing Blend, Reassuring Blend, Invigorating Blend, Joyful Blend, Kid's Restful Blend, Kid's Grounding Blend, Captivating Blend, Hopeful Blend

Supplements:

Copaifera Softgels

Additional Support:

Try adding in Copaifera Softgels twice daily. Inhale Vetiver directly from bottle or apply 2-3 drops over heart. Apply Hopeful Blend to palms of hands and deeply inhale for 5 breaths.

Protocol

» Diffuse 2 drops each of Grapefruit, Wild Orange, Lemon, and Bergamot.[82]

» Apply 3 drops Blue Tansy and Lemon onto cotton-wick inhaler and inhale deeply for multiple times per day (refresh with new oils every 5 days).[83]

» Apply Renewing Blend or Reassuring Blend over heart and deeply inhale aroma.

» Diffuse 3 drops each Invigorating Blend and Joyful Blend

» For Kids: Apply Kid's Restful Blend and Kid's Grounding Blend on chest, back of neck, and down the spine. Have child inhale directly from bottle for 5 deep breaths.

Suggested Duration:

Use daily as needed until feelings subside. Can use continually for as long as desired.

Gender Dysphoria

Oils and Blends:

Bergamot, Basil, Blue Tansy, Pink Pepper, Frankincense, Helichrysum, Lavender, Petitgrain, Litsea, Manuka, Rose, Magnolia, Roman Chamomile, Blend for Women, Focus Blend, Kid's Focus Blend, Fortifying Blend, Comforting Blend, Reassuring Blend

---

Additional Support:

Try applying Comforting Blend and Reassuring Blend over heart. Diffuse 2 drops Petitgrain, 2 drops Basil, and 2 drops Pink Pepper. Apply Focus blend or Kid's Focus blend on back of neck.

Protocol

» Apply Fortifying Blend or Blend for Women over heart.

» Sprinkle 3 drops each of Litsea, Manuka, and Bergamot onto cotton-wick inhaler and inhale deeply multiple times per day (refresh oils often). Or place 1 drop of each oil in palms and inhale deeply.

» Apply 1 drop each Helichrysum, Frankincense, and Lavender around navel.

» Diffuse 3 drops each of Roman Chamomile, Rose, and Pink Pepper.

Suggested Duration:

Use daily to support ongoing emotional balance and confidence in self. Use any protocols that feel supportive and helpful as long as needed.

Grief

Oils and Blends:

Melissa, Marjoram, Mānuka, Rose, Frankincense, Lemon, Geranium, Neroli, Cypress, Respiratory Blend, Comforting Blend, Renewing Blend, Centering Blend, Invigorating Blend, Joyful Blend

Supplements:

Restful Complex Softgels

Additional Support:

Try adding 3 drops Cypress to cotton-wick inhaler along with 3 drops Melissa, 2 drops Marjoram, and 2 drops Geranium. If experiencing "heaviness" over chest, apply 2-3 drops Respiratory Blend over lungs and place 2-3 drops in a diffuser. Apply Mānuka to the wrists.
Apply Renewing Blend over the heart and on the back of the neck. Take 1-3 capsules of Restful Complex Softgels 30 min before bed or to help with napping during the day in unable to sleep at night. Supporting a healthy immune system is an important part of grief recovery. Many of the above oils are chosen for both emotional properties and terpene content, which supports immune function.

Testimony/Story:

"I had an emotional support animal that was assigned to me after my tour in Iraq, and I unfortunately lost her to cancer. I went through a major depression and ultimately felt grief unlike anything I had ever known before. My dog, Major, was like the other half of me and I didn't know how to cope with her being gone. I ended up gravitating to using Melissa, Frankincense, Rose, Neroli, and Respiratory Blend in cycles over a period of about 3 months. I alternated between diffusing and using them topically over my heart. I used the one that called out to me daily, they helped to take the edge off, and after a few months I really did feel a lot better and I was ready to get a new emotional support dog that I named 'Major Blessing.'" - Samuel U.

Protocol

» Apply Comforting Blend or Centering Blend over heart or diffuse in room.

» Diffuse 3 drops each of Frankincense, Lemon, and Cypress during the day.[84]

» Apply 3 drops Melissa, 2 drops Marjoram, and 2 drops Geranium onto cotton-wick inhaler and inhale deeply multiple times per day (refresh oils often). Or place 1 drop of each oil in palms and inhale deeply. Can be done every 1-2 hours if needed.

» Apply 2 drops each of Rose, Frankincense, and Neroli to neck and massage into neck and shoulders with fractionated coconut oil 2-3 times daily (these oils may also be used in an aromatherapy inhaler).[85]

» Diffuse 3 drops each of Invigorating Blend and Joyful Blend.

Suggested Duration:

Use protocol daily while experiencing periods of grief. May benefit from daily use for 3-6 months or longer.

Guilt

Oils and Blends:

Bergamot, Copaiba, Ylang Ylang, Wild Orange, Black Pepper, Peppermint, Comforting Blend, Renewing Blend, Reassuring Blend, Respiratory Blend, Holiday Peaceful Blend

Supplements:

Fruit and Veggie Drink, Copaifera Softgels

Additional Support:

Try inhaling Black Pepper directly from the bottle for 5 deep breaths. Diffuse Respiratory Blend. Mix 1 drop Peppermint with 12 oz of water and drink. Guilt can have a detrimental effect on one's health, adding in 1 scoop of Fruit and Veggie drink in the morning can help support getting key nutrients and antioxidants.

Protocol

» Apply Comforting Blend and Renewing Blend over the heart and take 5 deep breaths.

» Diffuse Reassuring Blend or Holiday Peaceful Blend and deeply inhale aroma.

» Sprinkle 2 drops Bergamot, 1 drop Ylang Ylang, and 3 drops Wild Orange onto cotton-wick inhaler and inhale deeply multiple times per day (refresh oils often). Or place 1 drop of each oil in palms and inhale deeply.

» Take 1-2 Copaifera Softgels twice daily.

Suggested Duration:

Use for a minimum of 3 weeks, then ongoing as needed for support.

Have to be Right

Oils and Blends:

Cassia, Eucalyptus, Cinnamon, Frankincense, Grapefruit, Green Mandarin, Lemon, Vetiver, Ylang Ylang, Grounding Blend, Kid's Grounding Blend, Reassuring Blend, Restful Blend, Kid's Restful Blend

---

Additional Support:

Try applying Restful Blend or Kid's Restful Blend over heart and Grounding Blend or Kid's Grounding Blend on bottoms of feet. Sprinkle 3 drops each of Eucalyptus, Cassia, and Cinnamon onto cotton-wick inhaler and inhale deeply multiple times per day (refresh oils often). Or place 1 drop of each oil into diffuser. Consider Cognitive Behavior Therapy as mentioned in the foundational supports in the intro section in this book.

Protocol

» Apply Reassuring Blend over heart and deeply inhale.

» Diffuse 2 drops each Ylang Ylang, Grapefruit, and Frankincense and inhale deeply for 5 breaths.

» Sprinkle 3 drops each of Lemon, Vetiver, and Frankincense onto cotton-wick inhaler and inhale deeply multiple times per day (refresh oils often). Or place 1 drop of each oil in palms and inhale deeply.

Suggested Duration:

Use daily as needed when feeling rigid, stubborn, or unyielding. Diffuse regularly in tense situations.

Hate

Oils and Blends:

Roman Chamomile, Geranium, Ylang Ylang, Lavender, Lemon, Basil, Pink Pepper, Frankincense, Spearmint, Copaiba, Restful Blend, Kid's Restful Blend, Reassuring Blend, Comforting Blend, Renewing Blend, Cleansing Blend

Supplements:

Copaifera Softgels

Additional Support:

Try diffusing 2 drops each Roman Chamomile, Geranium, and Ylang Ylang. Apply Comforting Blend and Renewing Blend over heart. Also, see protocols for Betrayal, Embarrassed, Fear, Grief, Shame, or Sadness as these emotions can be underlying causes of hate.

Protocol

» Apply Reassuring Blend or Restful Blend or Kid's Restful Blend over heart.

» Take 2 drops Frankincense under tongue and 2 capsules Copaifera Softgels twice daily.

» Sprinkle 3 drops Basil, 2 drops Pink Pepper, and 10 drops Lemon onto cotton-wick inhaler and inhale deeply multiple times per day (refresh with new oils every 5 days). Or place 1 drop of each oil in palms and inhale deeply.

» Diffuse 4 drops Lemon and 2 drops Spearmint.[86]

» Apply Comforting Blend and Renewing Blend down spine.

» Diffuse Cleaning Blend to purify the environment energetically.

Suggested Duration:

Use daily for 1 month to fully release and dissipate these emotions from your body.

Hoarding

Oils and Blends:

Yarrow, Wintergreen, Wild Orange, Vetiver, Thyme, Siberian Fir, Rosemary, Rose, Magnolia, Lemon, Eucalyptus, Peppermint, Cleansing Blend, Joyful Blend, Comforting Blend, Inspiring Blend, Soothing Blend, Tension Blend

---

Additional Support:

Try applying Rose over heart and Magnolia on back of neck. Diffuse 2 drops each Thyme, Vetiver, and Siberian Fir. Inhale Rosemary directly from bottle. Apply 2 drops Yarrow over neck and decolletage, inhaling residual aroma left on hands for 4 deep breaths. Apply Tension Blend to back of neck.

Protocol

» Diffuse a mix of 4 drops each of Cleansing Blend and Joyful Blend.

» Alternate applying Comforting Blend and Inspiring Blend over heart.

» Inhale Wintergreen directly from bottle for 5 deep breaths.

» Sprinkle 3 drops each Eucalyptus, Peppermint, and Lemon onto cotton-wick inhaler, inhaling deeply for 5 breaths multiple times per day (refresh with oils every 3-7 days).[87] Or place 1 drop of each oil in palms and inhale deeply.

» Apply Soothing Blend to neck and shoulders to release emotional tension.

Suggested Duration:

Use daily to help create mental and emotional space to be able to clear out cluttered spaces. Use daily when physically clearing out clutter from spaces to support a healthy emotional state. Continue to use until both mental and physical space is cleared out.

Holding onto the Past

Oils and Blends:

Birch, Douglas Fir, Lime, Frankincense, Reassuring Blend, Comforting Blend, Renewing Blend, Enlightening Blend, Respiratory Blend

---

Additional Support:

Try applying Reassuring Blend over heart and taking 5 deep breaths. Diffuse Respiratory blend to open up airways and breathe new possibilities into life.

Testimony/Story:

"It broke my heart every time I went to visit my 83 year old grandmother when she would inevitably talk about an accident that occurred when she was 14 years old that ended up killing her 2 year old brother...I began setting up my diffuser at her home when I would come to visit and diffusing Douglas Fir, Lime, and Frankincense right next to her while we would visit. On the days I set up my diffuser she would not bring up the story... I was amazed that the oils seemed to create a pattern interrupt for her and allow us to talk about the present moment instead of dwelling on the past." - Karen R.

Protocol

» Diffuse 2 drops each Douglas Fir, Lime, Frankincense and place diffuser nearby.

» Apply Comforting Blend and Renewing Blend over heart and inhale deeply for 5 breaths.

» Apply Enlightening Blend on back of neck and diffuse it daily.

» Inhale Birch directly from bottle.

Suggested Duration:

Use daily as needed to move beyond the past.

Impatient

Oils and Blends:

Lavender, Lemon, Basil, Pink Pepper, Blue Tansy, Clary Sage, Bergamot, Wild Orange, Cypress, Frankincense, Lavender, Reassuring Blend, Restful Blend, Grounding Blend, Invigorating Blend, Joyful Blend, Grounding Blend

---

Additional Support:

Try sprinkling 2 drops Clary Sage, 2 drops Bergamot, and 4 drops Wild Orange onto cotton-wick inhaler and inhale deeply multiple times per day (refresh oils often). Or place 1 drop of each oil in palms and inhale deeply. Diffuse 2 drops each Blue Tansy and Lemon throughout the day or when feeling impatient. Diffuse a mix of 3 drops each of Invigorating Blend and Joyful Blend.

Protocol

» Apply 1-2 drops Reassuring Blend to palms of hands and deeply inhale for 5 deep breaths.

» Apply 1-2 drops Restful Blend over heart and on the back of the neck.

» Apply 2-3 drops Grounding Blend to wrists and bottoms of the feet.

» Diffuse 2 drops Basil, 3 drops Lavender, and 2 drops Pink Pepper to calm the nervous system and keep the mind alert.

» Diffuse 2 drops each of Cypress, Lavender, Frankincense, and Wild Orange throughout the day.

Suggested Duration:

Use daily as needed to support a relaxed, patient emotional state.

Insomnia

Oils and Blends:

Lavender, Petitgrain, Vetiver, Spikenard, Ylang Ylang, Magnolia, Sandalwood, Metabolic Blend, Restful Blend, Reassuring Blend, Kid's Restful Blend, Kid's Grounding Blend

Supplements:

Restful Complex Softgels

Additional Support:

Try applying Metabolic Blend to bottoms of feet. Diffuse 5 drops Petitgrain in room while falling asleep. Diffuse 5 drops Reassuring Blend in room while falling asleep and apply 1-2 drops over heart. Apply Magnolia to back of neck & deeply inhale aroma on hands.

Protocol

» Diffuse 2 drops Ylang Ylang, 3 drops Vetiver, and 2 drops Spikenard in room while falling asleep.[88]

» Spray sheets with mix of 4oz water & 10 drops Restful Blend.

» Take 1-3 capsules of Restful Complex Softgels 30 min before bed.

» Apply Sandalwood to bottoms of feet.

» For Kids: Apply Kid's Restful Blend and Kid's Grounding Blend to chest and bottoms of the feet. Diffuse Reassuring or Restful Blend in bedroom.

Suggested Duration:

Different protocols for sleep work for different people. Try one protocol at a time each night for a week, adding in the next protocol the following night to layer in topical application, aromatic diffusion, and internal use so that you are ultimately doing all 3 at night. Use nightly to help fall asleep once you find the right protocol for you.

Isolated

Oils and Blends:

Birch, Jasmine, Geranium, Frankincense, Peppermint, Myrrh, Sandalwood, Neroli, Douglas Fir, Lavender, Grounding Blend, Joyful Blend, Invigorating Blend, Encouraging Blend, Renewing Blend, Uplifting Blend, Holiday Joyful Blend

Additional Support:

Try adding 1 drop Ylang Ylang and 1 drop Geranium over the heart and breathe in deeply. Diffuse Holiday Joyful Blend. Apply Jasmine to back of neck. Diffuse a mix of 3 drops each of Joyful Blend and Invigorating Blend. Alternate applying Encouraging Blend and Renewing Blend over the heart throughout the day. Inhale Birch directly from bottle.

Protocol

» Diffuse 1 drop Geranium, 1 drop Ylang Ylang, and 2 drops Lavender.

» Rub 3-4 drops of Grounding Blend on bottom of each foot.

» Apply Inspiring Blend or Uplifting Blend over heart.

» Put 1 drop each of Neroli, Douglas Fir, and Wild Orange to palms of hands and deeply inhale.

» For feelings of Spiritual Isolation: Diffuse 2 drops Frankincense, 2 drops Sandalwood, and 2 drops Myrrh. Optional: Add 1 drop Rose to diffuser.

Suggested Duration:

Use daily as needed in an ongoing manner, or in moments of feeling intense isolation.

Jealousy

Oils and Blends:

Wild Orange, Geranium, Ylang Ylang, Basil, Pink Pepper, Eucalyptus, Grapefruit, Juniper Berry, Roman Chamomile, Lavender, Bergamot, Lemon, Frankincense, Inspiring Blend, Uplifting Blend, Encouraging Blend, Steadying Blend

---

Additional Support:

Try applying Uplifting Blend or Encouraging Blend over the heart. Diffuse 4 drops Eucalyptus and deeply inhale aroma. Diffuse 2 drops Basil, 3 drops Lavender, and 2 drops Pink Pepper to calm the nervous system and enhance self worth.

Protocol

» Apply Inspiring Blend over the heart.

» Diffuse Steadying Blend and deeply inhale aroma.

» Sprinkle 2 drops each of Ylang Ylang, Roman Chamomile, and Geranium onto cotton-wick inhaler and inhale deeply multiple times per day (refresh oils often). Or place 1 drop of each oil in palms and inhale deeply.

» Diffuse 2 drops each of Grapefruit, Wild Orange, Lemon, and Bergamot when feeling jealous.

Suggested Duration:

Use daily while experiencing feelings of jealousy. Continue to use as needed until feelings dissipate.

Lack of Boundaries

Oils and Blends:

Cinnamon, Cypress, Bergamot, Frankincense, Myrrh, Tea Tree, Cardamom, Marjoram, Douglas Fir, Siberian Fir, Lemongrass, Respiratory Blend, Inspiring Blend

---

Additional Support:

Try diffusing Respiratory Blend regularly to clear the airways and open up the mind to the possibility of change. Apply Inspiring Blend over the heart. Apply 1 drop Tea Tree to the wrists.

Protocol

» Diffuse 1 drop each of Cinnamon, Tea Tree, Cardamom, Lemongrass. This blend may be helpful setting boundaries with close friends and relationship partners.

» Diffuse 1 drop each Cypress, Bergamot, Douglas Fir or Siberian Fir. This blend may be helpful for breaking free from codependent behavior.

» Apply 2 drops each of Myrrh, Marjoram, and Frankincense to cotton-wick inhaler and inhale deeply multiple times per day (refresh oils often). Or place 1 drop of each oil in palms and inhale deeply. This blend may be helpful with setting boundaries with parents and immediate family members.

Suggested Duration:

Use for 2-3 months. Use these methods and protocols ongoing until relationship dynamics and patterns begin to shift in the areas of your life that you want to see change.

Limiting Beliefs

Oils and Blends:

Wild Orange, Basil, Pink Pepper, Eucalyptus, Grapefruit, Juniper Berry, Roman Chamomile, Sandalwood, Lavender, Lemon, Frankincense, Inspiring Blend, Uplifting Blend, Encouraging Blend, Anti-Aging Blend, Invigorating Blend, Captivating Blend, Detoxification Blend

---

Additional Support:

Try applying Anti-Aging Blend over heart. Place 1 drop each Frankincense and Sandalwood into palm of hands, rub together, and deeply inhale for 6 breaths. Diffuse 2 drops each of Grapefruit, Wild Orange, and Lemon Apply Captivating Blend to the wrists. Diffuse Detoxification Blend.

Testimony/Story:

"As an entrepreneur, I find myself overcoming limiting beliefs all the time! I diffuse these oils (Eucalyptus, Wild Orange, and Juniper Berry) whenever I needed to make a 'big leap' in my life or business. When I do, I feel a boost in confidence to go out and do the things that scare me... I also apply Uplifting Blend over my heart daily, and it makes a huge difference!" - Ruby Z.

Protocol

- » Apply Inspiring Blend over heart & deeply inhale for 5 breaths.
- » Diffuse Invigorating Blend or Uplifting Blend.
- » Place 1 drop of each oil, Eucalyptus, Wild Orange, Juniper Berry into palms and inhale.
- » Diffuse 2 drops each of Basil, Pink Pepper, and Roman Chamomile.[91]

Suggested Duration:

Use daily for 1 month, then ongoing as needed to overcome limiting beliefs.

Listless/Lost

Oils and Blends:

Lime, Blue Tansy, Lemon, Eucalyptus, Douglas Fir, Lemon, Wild Orange, Frankincense, Rosemary, Jasmine, Rose, Magnolia, Invigorating Blend, Joyful Blend

Additional Support:

If you're not seeing the results you'd like to see try these variances:
Sexually Lost: Apply Jasmine over heart and wrists.
Spiritually Lost: Apply Rose over heart and wrists. Diffuse 2 drops each of Blue Tansy and Lemon throughout the day or when feeling lost.

Testimony/Story:

"My whole life changed for the better when I started diffusting 3 drops each of Lime, Eucalyptus, and Douglas Fir everyday! I used to feel so lethargic about life. ... When I started diffusing that blend, I became curious, excited, and engaged with my life again. It literally breathed life back into me as I breathed in the vapor from my diffuser!" - Amanda S.

Protocol

» Apply 1 drop each Invigorating Blend and Joyful Blend into palms of hands and deeply inhale for 5 breaths.

» Diffuse 3 drops each of Lime, Eucalyptus, and Douglas Fir to support feeling grounded, uplifted, & having an appetite for life.

» Sprinkle 4 drops each of Frankincense and Basil onto cotton-wick inhaler and inhale deeply multiple times per day (refresh oils often). Or place 1 drop of each oil in palms and inhale.

Suggested Duration:

Use daily when feeling lost/listless to support healthy emotions and prevent negative emotions from dominating your day. Continue to use any protocols that feel supportive in an ongoing manner.

Lonely

Oils and Blends:

Thyme, Jasmine, Geranium, Ylang Ylang, Wild Orange, Frankincense, Neroli, Douglas Fir, Lavender, Grounding Blend, Joyful Blend, Invigorating Blend, Encouraging Blend, Renewing Blend, Uplifting Blend, Comforting Blend, Gathering Blend

---

Additional Support:

Try adding 1 drop Ylang Ylang and 1 drop Geranium over the heart and breathing in deeply. Apply Jasmine to back of neck. Diffuse a mix of 3 drops each Joyful Blend and Invigorating Blend. Apply Renewing Blend over the heart. Diffuse Comforting Blend and apply Encouraging Blend over the heart. Diffuse Gathering Blend.

Protocol

» Diffuse 1 drop Geranium, 1 drop Ylang Ylang, and 2 drops Lavender.

» Rub 3-4 drops of Grounding Blend on bottom of the feet.

» Apply Inspiring Blend or Uplifting Blend over heart.

» Apply 3 drops Thyme, 4 drops Wild Orange, and 2 drops Ylang Ylang, onto cotton-wick inhaler and inhale deeply multiple times per day (refresh oils often). Or place 1 drop of each oil in palms and inhale deeply. Can be done every 1-2 hours if needed.

» Apply 1 drop each of Neroli, Douglas Fir, and Wild Orange to palms of hands and inhale deeply.

Suggested Duration:

Use daily as needed, or in moments of loneliness.

Materialistic

Oils and Blends:

Magnolia, Jasmine, Rose, Wild Orange, Lemon, Douglas Fir, Grounding Blend, Invigorating Blend, Joyful Blend, Uplifting Blend, Reassuring Blend, Restful Blend, Anti-Aging Blend

---

Additional Support:

If you're not seeing the results you'd like to see, try diffusing 3 drops each of Invigorating Blend and Joyful Blend. Apply Uplifting Blend over heart. Apply Anti-Aging Blend to wrists.

Protocol

» Apply Rose over heart, Jasmine on back of neck, and Magnolia on wrists.

» Diffuse Reassuring Blend or Restful Blend and deeply inhale for 5 breaths.

» Sprinkle 3 drops each of Wild Orange, Lemon, and Douglas Fir onto cotton-wick inhaler and inhale deeply multiple times per day (refresh oils often). Or place 1 drop of each oil in palms and inhale deeply.

Suggested Duration:

Use daily as needed to create a more balanced emotional mood state.

Negative Family Patterns

Oils and Blends:

Basil, Blue Tansy, Cinnamon, Frankincense, Myrrh, Sandalwood, Siberian Fir, Douglas Fir, Cypress, Arborvitae, Lemon, Restful Blend, Kid's Restful Blend, Reassuring Blend, Holiday Peaceful Blend, Grounding Blend, Kid's Grounding Blend, Kid's Courage Blend

---

Additional Support:

Try diffusing Restful Blend. Apply 3 drops Douglas Fir, 3 drops Cypress, 3 drops Arborvitae, and 5 drops Lemon onto cotton-wick inhaler and inhale deeply multiple times per day (refresh oils often). Or simply place 1 drop of each oil in palms and inhale deeply. Can be done every 1-2 hours if needed. Rub Basil on the bottom of the feet.

Protocol

» Apply Comforting Blend or Renewing Blend over heart and inhale deeply for 5 breaths.

» Diffuse 2 drops Cinnamon, 3 drops Frankincense, and 3 drops Myrrh.

» Apply 3 drops Blue Tansy and Lemon onto cotton-wick inhaler and inhale deeply multiple times per day (refresh oils often). Or place 1 drop of each oil in palms and inhale deeply. Can be done every 1-2 hours if needed.

» For Kids with challenging home lives or who are displaced from family: Kid's Restful Blend and Kid's Grounding Blend applied to the back of neck, spine, and bottoms of the feet. Kid's Courage Blend applied over heart.

Suggested Duration:

Use daily while working on healing family patterns or use during therapy sessions. Use ongoing as needed when confronting or dealing with negative family dynamics.

Night Terrors

Oils and Blends:

Lavender, Petitgrain, Vetiver, Spikenard, Ylang Ylang, Magnolia, Sandalwood, Reassuring Blend, Restful Blend, Kid's Restful Blend, Kid's Grounding Blend

Supplements:

Restful Complex Softgels

Additional Support:

Try diffusing 2 drops Ylang Ylang, 2 drops Vetiver, each 4 drops Juniper Berry in room while falling asleep. Diffuse 5 drops Reassuring Blend in room while falling asleep and apply 1-2 drops over heart. Apply Magnolia to back of neck and deeply inhale aroma leftover on hands for 5 deep breaths. Diffuse 4 drops Petitgrain while falling asleep. Apply 1-2 drops Vetiver to pillow before bed.

Testimony/Story:

"All hail Juniper Berry and Restful Blend essential oils! My poor, sweet five-year-old son would wake up crying and screaming almost every night until we started diffusing Juniper Berry and rubbing his back with Restful Blend. These oils saved this mama's heart from hurting every night watching him suffer. Any parent who has a child with night terrors need to get these oils in your home!" - Anna P

Protocol

» Diffuse 4-6 drops Juniper Berry in room next to bed while falling asleep and keep diffusing for 6 hours.[92]

» Spray sheets with mixture of 4oz water and 10 drops Restful Blend (or simply apply 1-2 drops to pillow and sheets) to create a relaxing environment.[93]

» Take 1-3 capsules of Restful Complex Softgels 30 min before bed or to help with napping during the day if unable to sleep restfully at night.

» Apply Sandalwood to bottom of the feet.[94]

» For Kids: Apply Kid's Restful Blend and Kid's Grounding Blend to chest and bottom of the feet. Spray sheets with mixture of 4oz water and 10 drops Restful Blend. Diffuse 4 drops Reassuring Blend mixed with 4 drops Juniper Berry in bedroom, or just diffuse 4 drops Juniper Berry.

Suggested Duration:

Different things work for different people. Try one protocol at a time each night for a week, adding in the next protocol the following night to find what works best for you. Use nightly for 1 month minimum once you find a protocol that works for you.

Obsessive Compulsive Behavior

Oils and Blends:

Blue Tansy, Cilantro, Clary Sage, Sandalwood, Vetiver, Frankincense, Lemon, Marjoram, Myrrh, Grapefruit, Roman Chamomile, Lavender, Restful Blend, Reassuring Blend, Grounding Blend

Supplements:

Copaifera Softgels

Additional Support:

Try adding Copaifera Softgels twice daily. Diffuse 1 drop Clary Sage, 2 drops Lavender, 2 drops Marjoram, and 1 drop Roman Chamomile daily. Inhale Cilantro directly from bottle.

Testimony/Story:

"After dealing with a major hospitalization, I was having an extreme episode of obsessing over my health and stability. I had fallen down a few times after getting home from the hospital and I was obsessing over when and how I was going to fall again, needing to walk with a walker just to make it from the bedroom to the bathroom. My anxiety was through the roof! I was so focused on when I was going to fall next that I would unconsciously make my body tremble. My sister rubbed me down with Restful Blend on my wrists, back, and feet and within seconds my body stopped shaking enough to focus on taking steps and not falling down. Using these oils totally broke the pattern of the intrusive thoughts I was having, and allowed me to stop obsessing." - Bruce C.

Protocol

» Apply 1-3 drops Restful Blend to wrists and over heart.[95]

» Aromatherapy Inhaler Blend #1: Apply 2 drops Blue Tansy, 2 drops Vetiver, and 3 drops Grapefruit to cotton-wick inhaler and inhale deeply multiple times per day (refresh oils often). Or place 1 drop of each oil in palms and inhale deeply. Can be done every 1-2 hours if needed.

» Aromatherapy Inhaler Blend #2: Apply 3 drops Sandalwood, 4 drops Lemon, and 3 drops Frankincense to cotton-wick inhaler and inhale deeply multiple times per day (refresh oils often). Or place 1 drop of each oil in palms and inhale deeply. Can be done every 1-2 hours if needed.

» Apply Grounding Blend to bottoms of feet.

Suggested Duration:

1-2 months using daily or ongoing as needed until feelings subside.

Overeating

Oils and Blends:

Bergamot, Ylang Ylang, Geranium, Clary Sage, Fennel, Eucalyptus, Frankincense, Ginger, Jasmine, Lemon, Rosemary, Spearmint, Metabolic Blend, Digestive Blend, Renewing Blend, Invigorating Blend

Supplements:

Fruit and Veggie Drink

Additional Support:

Try sprinkling 3 drops each of Clary Sage and Eucalyptus onto cotton-wick inhaler and inhale deeply multiple times per day (refresh oils often). Or place 1 drop of each oil in palms and inhale deeply. Apply Jasmine over heart. Diffuse 5 drops Lemon, 2 drops Rosemary, 2 drops Spearmint. Take 1 scoop of Fruit and Veggie drink in the morning.

Testimony/Story:

"I have had a massive problem with food addiction and overeating my whole life. If I felt anxious, sad, happy, proud, lonely, excited, successful---I ate! No matter what the occasion I made food my sidekick. After starting to use Metabolic Blend 2-3 times daily in my water and inhaling oils to support my moods instead of reaching for foods first, I have been losing weight and I have stopped feeling resentment towards myself when I look in the mirror. I am a new woman because of these oils." - Ramona E.

Protocol

» Diffuse 3 drops Bergamot, 2 drops Ylang Ylang, and 2 drops Geranium to support love and appreciation of the body.

» Apply Renewing Blend over heart and deeply inhale for 5 breaths.

» Inhale Fennel directly from the bottle or apply 1 drop Fennel to tongue to soothe intense cravings.

» Drink 12 oz of water with 2 drops Metabolic Blend to inhibit binging episodes and support healthy blood sugar levels.

» Apply 2 drops Digestive Blend around naval or drink 1 drop in 4 oz of water to reduce nausea, feelings of discomfort in the stomach, or purging behaviors.

» Diffuse 3 drops each of Frankincense, and Ginger or Invigorating Blend to uplift mood.

Suggested Duration:

Use daily or as needed to ward off unwanted food habits and behaviors. Continue to use daily to support mental peace around food.

Over Serious

Oils and Blends:

Lemon, Lime, Grapefruit, Bergamot, Douglas Fir, Eucalyptus, Invigorating Blend, Uplifting Blend, Holiday Peaceful Blend, Inspiring Blend, Kid's Courage Blend

---

Additional Support:

Try diffusing Invigorating Blend or Holiday Peaceful Blend and applying Kid's Courage Blend over heart. Apply Inspiring Blend to wrists.

Testimony/Story:

"I have a 5 year old who ... tends to take everything so seriously and personally and has a hard time laughing at himself. We love to diffuse Grapefruit, Wild Orange, Lemon, and Bergamot as the 'liquid sunshine' blend on our home! It immediately brightens my son's day and his mood and makes us both smile." - Laura V.

Protocol

» Diffuse 4-5 drops of Uplifting Blend throughout the day to lighten the mood.

» Sprinkle 2 drops each of Grapefruit, Wild Orange, Lemon, and Bergamot onto cotton-wick inhaler and inhale deeply multiple times per day (refresh oils often). Or place 1 drop of each oil in palms and inhale deeply.

» Diffuse 3 drops each of Lime, Eucalyptus, and Douglas Fir to support feeling light-hearted and having an appetite for life.

Suggested Duration:

Use as needed. Diffuse on a daily basis if it is a chronic problem.

Over Stimulated

Oils and Blends:

Ylang Ylang, Roman Chamomile, Lavender, Tangerine, Wild Orange, Lemon, Grapefruit, Vetiver, Copaiba, Frankincense, Cedarwood, Sandalwood, Spikenard, Reassuring Blend, Restful Blend, Grounding Blend, Kid's Restful Blend, Kid's Grounding Blend, Hopeful Blend

Supplements:

Restful Complex Softgels, Copaifera Softgels

Additional Support:

Try diffusing 6-7 drops Frankincense. Diffuse 2 drops each of Grapefruit, Wild Orange, Lemon, and Tangerine. Apply Cedarwood to bottoms of feet and Sandalwood down the spine and back of the neck. Take Restful Complex Softgels 30 min prior to sleep.

Protocol

» Diffuse Restful Blend nearby and inhale deeply as it diffuses.[96]

» Apply Reassuring Blend over heart and take 5 deep breaths.

» Take 2 Copaifera Softgels twice daily.

» Or place 1 drop of each, Frankincense, Roman Chamomile, and Lavender in palms and inhale deeply.[97]

» For Kids: Apply Reassuring Blend over heart, Kid's Restful Blend to back of neck, and Kid's Grounding Blend to feet. Diffuse Reassuring Blend.

Suggested Duration:

Use daily as needed to prevent and combat feelings of overstimulation.

Parasitic Relationships

Oils and Blends:

Basil, Lavender, Cinnamon, Cypress, Bergamot, Frankincense, Myrrh, Cardamom, Marjoram, Roman Chamomile, Douglas Fir, Siberian Fir, Grapefruit, Clove Bud, Lemongrass, Inspiring Blend, Reassuring Blend, Comforting Blend, Kid's Courage Blend, Soothing Blend, Protective Blend

Additional Support:

Try sprinkling 2 drops Clove Bud, 6 drops Grapefruit, 2 drops Roman Chamomile to cotton-wick inhaler and inhale deeply multiple times per day (refresh oils often) If you don't have inhaler put 1 drop of each oil in a diffuser. Diffuse regularly. This blend may be helpful with establishing boundaries and help with confidence, grace, and calmness. Inhale Wintergreen oil directly from the bottle. Apply Soothing Blend to neck and shoulders to release emotional tension. Diffuse Protective Blend.

Protocol

» Apply Kid's Courage Blend, Reassuring Blend, or Comforting blend over the heart.

» Apply 2 drops Basil, 3 drops Lavender, and 3 drops Lime to diffuser and deeply inhale while sitting next to it. Or apply 1 drop of each to palms of hands and deeply inhale for 5 deep breaths. This blend may help with confidently speaking your needs and advocating for self.

» Diffuse 1 drop each of Cinnamon, Tea Tree, Cardamom, Lemongrass. This blend may be helpful with breaking free from parasitic bonds with close friends and romantic partners.

» Diffuse 1 drop each Cypress, Bergamot, Douglas Fir or Siberian Fir. This blend may be helpful for breaking free from codependent behavior with others in general.

» Apply 2 drops each of Myrrh, Marjoram, and Frankincense to cotton-wick inhaler and inhale deeply multiple times per day (refresh oils often). Or place 1 drop of each oil in palms and inhale deeply. Can be done every 1-2 hours if needed. This blend may be helpful with breaking free from parasitic bonds with parents and immediate family members.

Suggested Duration:

Use for 2-3 months. Use these methods and protocols ongoing until relationship dynamics and patterns begin to shift in the areas of your life you want to see them change.

Panic Disorder

Oils and Blends:

Basil, Blue Tansy, Copaiba, Cedarwood, Fennel, Frankincense, Geranium, Grapefruit, Jasmine, Lavender, Lemon, Marjoram, Melissa, Neroli, Pink Pepper, Roman Chamomile, Rose, Rosemary, Spearmint, Tangerine, Vetiver, Wild Orange, Ylang Ylang, Reassuring Blend, Restful Blend, Kid's Restful Blend, Grounding Blend, Kid's Grounding Blend, Kid's Courage Blend, Steadying Blend, Enlightening Blend

Supplements:

Restful Complex Softgels, Copaifera Softgels

Additional Support:

Try diffusing 3 drops each of Lemon, Marjoram, and Lavender. Apply Steadying Blend or Enlightening Blend over heart. Sprinkle 3 drops Vetiver, 4 drops Wild Orange, and 4 drops Frankincense onto cotton-wick inhaler and inhale deeply multiple times per day (refresh oils often). Or place 1 drop of each oil in palms and inhale deeply. Diffuse 2 drops each of Melissa, Geranium, and Cedarwood. Apply Rose, Jasmine, or Neroli over heart and deeply inhale for 5 breaths. Diffuse 3 drops each Tangerine and Pink Pepper. Take Restful Complex Softgels prior to situations that have caused panic historically. Take 2 Copaifera Softgels twice daily.

Testimony/Story:

"I have had panic issues my entire life and my whole family has a long lineage of them as well. I used to feel like I was going to have a heart attack and die, or get feelings of imminent danger and bodily harm for no reason and I couldn't logically talk myself out of it. Now, I just reach for my aromatherapy inhaler or the two oils I always carry in my pocket- Reassuring Blend and Restful Blend- and within moments my body relaxes and reprograms to "safe" without me having to logically justify in my mind why I am ok. It works so quickly and effectively--it's been a tremendous lifesaver to me. I no longer feel powerless." - Cameron D.

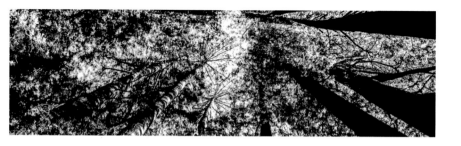

Protocol

» Apply Restful Blend of Kid's Restful Blend over heart and take 5 deep breaths.[98]

» Apply Grounding Blend or Kid's Grounding Blend on bottom of the feet.

» Sprinkle 3 drops Ylang Ylang, 3 drops Roman Chamomile, and 7 drops Grapefruit onto cotton-wick inhaler and inhale deeply multiple times per day (refresh oils often).[99] Or place 1 drop of each oil in palms and inhale deeply.

» Diffuse 3 drops Blue Tansy and 4 drops Lemon.[100]

» Inhale Basil directly from the bottle.[101]

Suggested Duration:

Use daily for one week to continue to relax the mind and emotional state even after the feelings of episodic panic subside. Continue to use as needed to support positive mood state.

Paranoia

Oils and Blends:

Clove Bud, Copaiba, Eucalyptus, Frankincense, Geranium, Grapefruit, Helichrysum, Lavender, Lemon, Melissa, Peppermint, Roman Chamomile, Rose, Rosemary, Basil, Spearmint, Spikenard, Vetiver, Wild Orange, Ylang Ylang, Steadying Blend, Restful Blend, Reassuring Blend

Supplements:

Copaifera Softgels

Additional Support:

Try sprinkling 2 drops Clove Bud, 6 drops Grapefruit, 2 drops Roman Chamomile to cotton-wick inhaler and inhale deeply multiple times per day (refresh oils often) If you don't have inhaler put 1 drop of each oil in a diffuser. Diffuse regularly. Inhale Basil directly from the bottle. Sprinkle 1 drop Geranium, 1 drop Melissa, 1 drop Ylang Ylang, and 3 drops Frankincense onto cotton-wick inhaler and inhale deeply multiple times per day (refresh oils often). Or place 1 drop of each oil in palms and inhale deeply. Can be done every 1-2 hours if needed.

Testimony/Story:

"My dad has struggled with paranoia his whole life. It's caused major issues in our family because of it. I notice that when we diffuse oils ongoing everyday he's much better. He even started bringing his own inhaler to work with him and is having less issues at work." - B.A.

Protocol

» Diffuse Steadying Blend or Restful Blend to relax the mind.

» Take 2 Copaifera Softgels twice daily to stabilize mood and relax the body.

» Apply 3 drops Vetiver or Reassuring Blend over heart and deeply inhale for 5-6 breaths.

» Diffuse 2 drops each of Spearmint, Wild Orange, and Peppermint.

» Apply 3 drops Lemon, 2 drops Rose, and 3 drops Eucalyptus to cotton-wick inhaler and inhale deeply multiple times per day (refresh oils often). Or place 1 drop of each oil in palms and inhale deeply. Can be done every 1-2 hours if needed.

» Sprinkle 2 drops each of Ylang Ylang, Spikenard, and Helichrysum onto cotton-wick inhaler and inhale deeply multiple times per day (refresh oils often).[102] Or place 1 drop of each oil in hands and inhale deeply.

» Put 1 drop of Melissa oil to thumb and press it to the roof of the mouth, holding for 15 seconds.[103]

Suggested Duration:

Use daily as a preventative measure in an ongoing basis. Use as needed in moments of paranoia.

Parkinson's Disease

Oils and Blends:

Clove Bud, Copaiba, Coriander, Cinnamon, Cardamom, Lemon, Grapefruit, Roman Chamomile, Sandalwood, Basil, Frankincense, Grounding Blend, Wild Orange, Cellular Complex Blend, Restful Blend, Kid's Restful Blend

Supplements:

Cellular Complex Softgel, Copaifera Softgels, Restful Complex Softgel

---

Additional Support:

Try diffusing 2 drops Coriander, 2 drops Basil, and 2 drops Lemon for a mentally energizing aroma. Diffuse 2 drops Cinnamon, 3 drops Wild Orange and 3 drops Cardamom for neuroprotective, uplifting blend. Take Restful Complex Softgels 30 min prior to bed.

Protocol

» Apply Restful Blend or Kid's Restful Blend on back of neck to relax and ease any feelings of uneasiness.

» Diffuse 2 drops Clove Bud, 6 drops Grapefruit, 2 drops Roman Chamomile for relaxing, uplifting, and neuroprotective properties of blend.[104]

» Take 2 Cellular Complex Softgels and 2 Copaifera Softgels twice daily for brain and nerve support.

» Massage 1 drop each of Frankincense and Sandalwood into hands and gently massage any areas that have tremors or shakiness.

» Apply Grounding Blend to bottom of the feet and over heart.

Suggested Duration:

Use daily for neuroprotective support, uplifting the mood, and relaxing the nervous system.

Perfectionism

Oils and Blends:

Clary Sage, Bergamot, Wild Orange, Cypress, Frankincense, Lavender, Ylang Ylang, Grapefruit, Reassuring Blend, Restful Blend, Grounding Blend, Invigorating Blend, Joyful Blend

---

Additional Support:

If you're not yet seeing the results you'd like to see, try diffusing Ylang Ylang, Grapefruit and Frankincense and inhale deeply for 5 breaths. Try experimenting with different citrus oils such as Lemon, Lime, Grapefruit, Tangerine, Bergamot, Invigorating Blend, or Joyful Blend in your diffuser to achieve the results that feel best in your body for alleviating perfectionistic tendencies.

Protocol

» Apply 1-2 drops Reassuring Blend to palms of hands and deeply inhale for 4 deep breaths.

» Apply 1-2 drops Restful Blend over heart and on back of neck.

» Apply 2-3 drops Grounding Blend to wrists & bottom of feet.

» Sprinkle 2 drops Clary Sage, 2 drops Bergamot, and 4 drops Wild Orange onto cotton-wick inhaler and carry with you, inhaling deeply for 5 breaths multiple times per day (refresh oils often). Or place 1 drop of each oil in palms and inhale from hands.

» Diffuse 2 drops each of Cypress, Lavender, Frankincense, and Wild Orange throughout the day.

Suggested Duration:

Use ongoing as needed as long as feelings of perfectionism continue. Use one or more of the protocols mentioned as needed to support a balanced mood state.

Pessimism

Oils and Blends:

Rose, Clary Sage, Lime, Grapefruit, Lemon, Lavender, Petitgrain, Comforting Blend, Renewing Blend, Reassuring Blend

Supplements:

Copaifera Softgels

Additional Support:

Try applying 2 drops Rose, 2 drops Clary Sage, 2 drops Petitgrain to cotton-wick inhaler and inhale deeply multiple times per day (refresh oils often). Or place 1 drop of each oil in palms and inhale deeply. Can be done every 1-2 hours if needed. Try applying Comforting Blend or Renewing blend over the heart.

Protocol

» Diffuse 2 drops each of Lemon, Lime, and Grapefruit to liven the heart.

» Apply Reassuring Blend over the heart to promote feelings of safety and comfort.

» Apply 2 drops Rose, 2 drops Clary Sage, and 3 drops Lavender to cotton-wick inhaler and inhale deeply multiple times per day (refresh oils often). Or place 1 drop of each oil in palms and inhale deeply. Can be done every 1-2 hours if needed.

Suggested Duration:

Use daily for one month. Use any methods above daily to support a healthy, balanced mind or to pull a person out of an episode of pessimistic feelings.

Phobias

Oils and Blends:

Clove Bud, Copaiba, Eucalyptus, Frankincense, Grapefruit, Helichrysum, Lavender, Lemon, Melissa, Peppermint, Roman Chamomile, Rose, Rosemary, Basil, Spearmint, Spikenard, Vetiver, Wild Orange, Ylang Ylang, Steadying Blend, Restful Blend, Reassuring Blend

Supplements:

Copaifera Softgels, Restful Blend Softgels

Additional Support:

Try diffusing 2 drops Clove Bud, 6 drops Grapefruit, and 2 drops Roman Chamomile. Inhale Basil directly from the bottle. Take Restful Blend Softgels during the day when feeling phobic or at night before bed to help get restful sleep.

Protocol

» Diffuse Steadying Blend or Restful Blend to calm body & mind.

» Take 2 Copaifera Softgels twice daily to relax & soothe body.

» Apply 3 drops Vetiver or Reassuring Blend over heart and deeply inhale.[105]

» Diffuse 2 drops of Spearmint, Wild Orange, & Peppermint.[106]

» Place 1 drop of each, Lemon, Rose and Eucalyptus, in palms and inhale deeply. Can be done every 1-2 hours if needed.

» Sprinkle 2 drops each of Ylang Ylang, Spikenard, and Helichrysum onto cotton-wick inhaler and inhale deeply multiple times per day (refresh oils often).[107]

» Put 1 drop of Melissa oil to thumb and press it to the roof of the mouth and hold for 15 seconds.

Suggested Duration:

Use daily as a preventative measure in an ongoing basis. Use as needed in moments of paranoia.

Prideful

Oils and Blends:

Cassia, Eucalyptus, Cinnamon, Frankincense, Grapefruit, Green Mandarin, Lemon, Vetiver, Ylang Ylang, Grounding Blend, Kid's Grounding Blend, Reassuring Blend, Restful Blend, Kid's Restful Blend

---

Additional Support:

Try applying Restful Blend or Kid's Restful Blend over heart and Grounding Blend or Kid's Grounding Blend on bottom of the feet. Sprinkle 3 drops each of Eucalyptus, Cassia, and Cinnamon onto cotton-wick inhaler and inhale deeply multiple times per day (refresh oils often). Or place 1 drop of each oil in palms and inhale deeply.

Protocol

» Apply Reassuring Blend over heart and deeply inhale.

» Diffuse Ylang Ylang, Grapefruit, and Frankincense and inhale deeply for 5 breaths.

» Sprinkle 3 drops each of Lemon, Frankincense, and Green Mandarin onto cotton-wick inhaler and inhale deeply multiple times per day (refresh oils often). Or place 1 drop of each oil in palms and inhale deeply.

Suggested Duration:

Use daily as needed when feeling prideful. Diffuse regularly in tense situations.

Psychosis/Psychotic Episodes

Oils and Blends:

Copaiba, Eucalyptus, Frankincense, Geranium, Grapefruit, Helichrysum, Lavender, Lemon, Melissa, Peppermint, Roman Chamomile, Rose, Rosemary, Basil, Spearmint, Spikenard, Vetiver, Wild Orange, Ylang Ylang, Steadying Blend, Restful Blend, Reassuring Blend

Supplements:

Copaifera Softgels

Additional Support:

Try diffusing 2 drops each of Spearmint, Wild Orange, and Peppermint or diffusing 2 drops Clove Bud, 6 drops Grapefruit, and 2 drops Roman Chamomile. Place 1 drop of each oil, Geranium, Melissa, Ylang Ylang and Frankincense in palms and inhale deeply. Inhale Basil directly from the bottle.

Protocol

» Diffuse Steadying Blend or Restful Blend.

» Take 2 Copaifera Softgels twice daily.

» Apply 3 drops Vetiver or Reassuring Blend over heart and deeply inhale for 5-6 breaths.

» Place 1 drop of each oil, Lemon, Rose and Eucalyptus in hands and inhale deeply.[108]

» Sprinkle 2 drops each of Ylang Ylang, Spikenard, and Helichrysum onto cotton-wick inhaler and inhale deeply multiple times per day (refresh oils often).[109]

» Put 1 drop of Melissa oil to thumb and press it to the roof of the mouth, holding for 15 seconds.[110]

Suggested Duration:

Use daily as a preventative measure. Use as needed in moments of delusion.

Post Traumatic Stress Disorder

Oils and Blends:

Basil, Pink Pepper, Cedarwood, Copaiba, Clary Sage, Eucalyptus, Fennel, Frankincense, Helichrysum, Jasmine, Juniper Berry, Lavender, Rosemary, Lemon, Lime, Magnolia, Melissa, Neroli, Patchouli, Roman Chamomile, Rose, Spearmint, Spikenard, Wild Orange, Ylang Ylang, Comforting Blend, Restful Blend, Joyful Blend

Supplements:

Restful Complex Softgels, Copaifera Softgels

Additional Support:

Try adding 1 drop Melissa oil to thumb and pressing to roof of mouth for 30 seconds. Try sprinkling 2 drops each of Ylang Ylang, Spikenard, and Helichrysum onto cotton-wick inhaler and inhale deeply multiple times per day (refresh oils often). Or place 1 drop of each oil in palms and inhale deeply. Diffuse 2 drops Rosemary and 3 drops Juniper Berry to inhale during therapy sessions. Apply 2 drops each of Juniper Berry, Rosemary, and Patchouli onto cotton-wick inhaler and inhale deeply multiple times per day (refresh oils often). This aromatherapy inhaler blend may be useful to use while in therapy sessions or while journaling and reprocessing events. Apply Joyful Blend over the heart. Take 1-3 capsules Restful Complex Softgels 30 min before bed.

Testimony/Story:

"I struggled with the crushing weight of an abusive past that, although it happened years ago, still haunts me to this day. It affects my relationships, my self worth, and my ability to confidently move forward with my future. I have even been to 10 years of therapy for it. When I began to use oils for my memories of abuse, and it was like a new space in my body opened up. I felt light where before it felt heavy. I felt space where before I had felt pressure. I felt relaxed where before I felt a ball of knots. Diffusing Lime, Wild Orange, and Spearmint daily as well as applying Comforting Blend over my heart always carries me through my rough days. Nowadays, I am feeling much better overall and my 'bad days' don't last as long. I wouldn't be where I am without these oils."
- Kandace S.

Protocol

» Alternate diffusing 4-6 drops Restful Blend and 5-6 drops Frankincense in diffuser throughout the day and place diffuser in close proximity to you.[111]

» Apply Comforting Blend or Restful Blend over the heart and deeply inhale aroma for 5 breaths.

» Take 2 drops Frankincense under tongue and 2 capsules Copaifera Softgels twice daily.

» Sprinkle 2 drops each of Clary Sage, Roman Chamomile, and Pink Pepper onto cotton-wick inhaler and inhale deeply multiple times per day (refresh oils often). Or place 1 drop of each oil in palms and inhale deeply.

» Apply Jasmine, Magnolia, and Neroli to the spine, back of the neck, or bottom of the feet.[112]

» Diffuse 2 drops each of Wild Orange, Lime, and Spearmint.

Suggested Duration:

Use daily for 3 months. Continue to use ongoing as needed to support a relaxed emotional state.

Purposeless

Oils and Blends:

Birch, Lime, Blue Tansy, Lemon, Eucalyptus, Douglas Fir, Lemon, Wild Orange, Frankincense, Rosemary, Jasmine, Rose, Invigorating Blend, Joyful Blend, Focus Blend, Kid's Focus Blend, Gathering Blend, Captivating Blend

---

Additional Support:

Try these variances: Apply 1 drop Frankincense on forehead and rub into temples. Apply Jasmine and Rose over heart. Diffuse 3 drops each of Invigorating Blend and Joyful Blend. Apply Focus Blend or Kid's Focus Blend to back of neck. Inhale Birch directly from bottle. Diffuse Gathering Blend.

Testimony/Story:

"I work as a writer for TV and whenever I am between writing gigs I feel this deep sense of lack of purpose. ... I started using Focus Blend on the back of my neck and diffusing Lime and Eucalyptus in my office and the combo of those oils re-energize my mind and I regain my sense of purpose." - Allen T.

Protocol

» Apply Inspiring Blend over heart and deeply inhale.

» Diffuse 3 drops each of Lime, Eucalyptus, and Douglas Fir to support feeling grounded, uplifted, and an appetite for life.

» Sprinkle 4 drops each of Frankincense and Basil onto cotton-wick inhaler and inhale deeply multiple times per day (refresh oils often). Or place 1 drop of each oil in palms and inhale.

» Apply Captivating Blend to palms, deeply inhale for 5 breaths.

Suggested Duration:

Use daily when feeling lost/listless to support healthy emotions and prevent negative emotions from dominating your day. Continue to use any protocols that feel supportive in an ongoing manner.

Rage

Oils and Blends:

Lavender, Frankincense, Lemon, Peppermint, Roman Chamomile, Bergamot, Geranium, Rosemary, Grapefruit, Orange, Cleansing Blend, Comforting Blend, Renewing Blend, Courage Blend

Supplements:

Vitality Supplement Trio, Fruit and Veggie Drink

Additional Support:

Try applying Courage Blend into palms of hands and deeply inhaling for 5 breaths. Diffuse either the Comforting or Renewing Blend instead of the above recipe. Take Vitality Supplement Trio twice daily to support whole-body health. Anger can deplete the body of nutrients and the body could need the extra support of vitamins, minerals, and antioxidants to help transition out of angry feelings permanently. Try one scoop Fruit and Veggie Drink for nutrient support.

Protocol

» Diffuse 2 drops of Grapefruit, Wild Orange, Lemon, and Bergamot in tense environments or when feeling angry.[113]

» Apply 1 drop each of Peppermint & Geranium over heart.[114]

» Apply 1 drop each Frankincense, Roman Chamomile and Lavender on to the spine. Inhale Peppermint or Rosemary directly from the bottle to reboot and refresh the mind.

» Diffuse Cleansing Blend to purify the environment energetically.

Suggested Duration:

Use as needed. Use daily for up to 1 month if anger is chronic. Continue using any protocols that support moving beyond feelings of rage and onto a secondary emotion that may need healing like sadness, fear, shame, guilt, etc. See protocols for Sadness, Fear, Shame and Guilt.

Reclusive

Oils and Blends:

Thyme, Jasmine, Geranium, Ylang Ylang, Wild Orange, Frankincense, Peppermint, Myrrh, Sandalwood, Neroli, Douglas Fir, Lavender, Grounding Blend, Joyful Blend, Invigorating Blend, Encouraging Blend, Renewing Blend, Uplifting Blend

---

Additional Support:

Try adding 1 drop Ylang Ylang and 1 drop Geranium over the heart and breathing in deeply. Apply Jasmine to back of neck. Diffuse a 3 drops each Joyful Blend and Invigorating Blend. Alternate applying Encouraging Blend and Renewing Blend over heart throughout day.

Testimony/Story:

"Neroli is my secret weapon against wanting to stay inside all day everyday. I inhale it from my hands and it makes me feel confident, brave, and energized." - Edgar G.

Protocol

» Diffuse 1 drop Geranium, 1 drop Ylang Ylang, and 2 drops Lavender.

» Rub 3-4 drops Grounding Blend on bottom of the feet.

» Apply Inspiring Blend over heart to inspire new possibilities.

» Diffuse Uplifting Blend to elevate mood.

» Apply 3 drops Thyme, 4 drops Wild Orange, and 2 drops Ylang Ylang, onto cotton-wick inhaler and inhale deeply multiple times per day (refresh oils often). Or place 1 drop of each oil in palms and inhale. Can be done every 1-2 hours if needed.

» Apply 1 drop each Neroli, Douglas Fir, and Wild Orange to palms of hands and deeply inhale.

Suggested Duration:

Use daily as needed in an ongoing manner or in moments of reclusivity, or while feeling intense isolation.

Regret

Oils and Blends:

Bergamot, Copaiba, Ylang Ylang, Wild Orange, Black Pepper, Peppermint, Comforting Blend, Renewing Blend, Reassuring Blend, Respiratory Blend

Supplements:

Fruit and Veggie Drink, Copaifera Softgels

Additional Support:

Try inhaling Black Pepper directly from the bottle for 5 deep breaths. Diffuse Respiratory Blend. Mix 1 drop Peppermint with 12 oz water and drink. Guilt can have a detrimental effect on one's health so adding in 1 scoop of Fruit and Veggie drink in the morning can help support getting key nutrients and antioxidants.

Protocol

» Apply Comforting Blend and Renewing Blend over the heart and take 5 deep breaths.

» Diffuse Reassuring Blend and deeply inhale aroma.

» Sprinkle 2 drops Bergamot, 1 drop Ylang Ylang, and 3 drops Wild Orange onto cotton-wick inhaler and inhale deeply multiple times per day (refresh oils often). Or place 1 drop of each oil in palms and inhale deeply.

» Take 1-2 Copaifera Softgels twice daily.

Suggested Duration:

Use for 3 weeks minimum. Use ongoing as needed for support to fully overcome feelings of regret.

Resentment

Oils and Blends:

Thyme, Jasmine, Geranium, Ylang Ylang, Wild Orange, Frankincense, Peppermint, Myrrh, Sandalwood, Neroli, Douglas Fir, Lavender, Grounding Blend, Joyful Blend, Invigorating Blend, Encouraging Blend, Renewing Blend, Uplifting Blend

Supplements:

Fruit and Veggie Drink, Polyphenol Complex

Additional Support:

Try diffusing 2 drops Rose and 1 drop Pink Pepper. Apply Renewing blend over heart. Diffuse Holiday Joyful Blend. Diffuse 1 drop each of Roman Chamomile and Vetiver. Take 1 scoop Fruit and Veggie drink in the morning to set the tone for a nourishing, positive day. Take 2 capsules Polyphenol Complex to reduce inflammation caused by intense negative feelings.

Protocol

» Diffuse 1-2 drops each of Spearmint, Frankincense, and Myrrh.

» Apply 1 drop each Siberian Fir, Douglas Fir, Helichrysum over the heart. Cup hands over nose with remaining oil on hands and inhale 5 deep breaths.

» Apply Comforting Blend on the back of the neck.

» Diffuse 3 drops of Reassuring blend or Gathering Blend.

Suggested Duration:

Use daily for 3 weeks minimum. Allow time to pass to process out the feelings of resentment as there may be layers of it like an onion being peeled back.

Resignation

Oils and Blends:

Frankincense, Copaiba, Peppermint, Rosemary, Blue Tansy, Lemon, Inspiring Blend, Uplifting Blend, Encouraging Blend, Invigorating Blend, Joyful Blend, Enlightening Blend

Supplements:

Copaifera Softgels

Additional Support:

Try diffusing Peppermint and Rosemary together in equal parts. Take 2 drops each of Frankincense and Copaiba together internally.

Protocol

» 2 drops Frankincense or Copaiba under the tongue twice daily, or take Copaifera Softgels twice daily.

» Diffuse Invigorating Blend or Joyful Blend, or a combination of the two oils.

» Apply 3 drops each of Blue Tansy and Lemon onto cotton-wick inhaler and inhale deeply multiple times per day (refresh oils often). Or place 1 drop of each oil in palms and inhale deeply. Can be done every 1-2 hours if needed.

» Diffuse 2-3 drops Enlightening Blend.

» Apply Inspiring Blend, Uplifting Blend, or Encouraging Blend essential oil blends over heart. Deeply inhale aroma for 5 breaths.

Suggested Duration:

Use for 1 week consecutively. Continue 1-3 above methods daily for as long as needed.

Rejection

Oils and Blends:

Bergamot, Black Pepper, Rose, Frankincense, Geranium, Lemon, Litsea, Neroli, Melissa, Roman Chamomile, Cypress, Peppermint, Rosemary, Grapefruit, Wintergreen, Respiratory Blend, Centering Blend, Reassuring Blend, Enlightening Blend, Holiday Peaceful Blend, Soothing Blend, Tension Blend

Supplements:

Restful Complex Softgels

Additional Support:

Try sprinkling 2 drops each of Frankincense, Roman Chamomile, and Lavender onto cotton-wick inhaler and inhale deeply multiple times per day (refresh oils often). Or place 1 drop of each oil in palms and inhale deeply. Add in Restful Complex Softgels before bedtime. Or try adding 3 drops Cypress to cotton-wick inhaler along with 3 drops Melissa, 2 drops Marjoram, and 2 drops Geranium. Diffuse 3 drops each of Frankincense, Lemon, and Cypress during the day. Apply 1 drop each Peppermint and Geranium over the heart and deeply inhale aroma for 5 breaths. Apply Soothing Blend to neck and shoulders to relieve emotional tension.

Testimony/Story:

"My daughter was engaged to be married and her wedding in three months out. The week before the wedding, her fiance called it off because he was hired for a high security job in the military and he wanted to live his life solo. My daughter was devastated and feeling so rejected. My mama heart wanted to fix it but knew I couldn't. Instead, I got out my oils and rubbed her back with Frankincense, Roman Chamomile, and Lavender, and diffused lots of citrus oils to keep her mood elevated. She's doing a lot better now, and I feel better as a mom having something I can do when I feel helpless to fix it!" - Alaina Z.

Protocol

» Alternate between applying Reassuring Blend and Respiratory blend over the heart throughout the day.

» Diffuse 2 drops each of Grapefruit, Wild Orange, Lemon, and Bergamot to lighten mood.

» Apply 3 drops Melissa, 2 drops Marjoram, 1 drop Litsea, and 2 drops Geranium onto cotton-wick inhaler and inhale deeply multiple times per day (refresh oils often). Or place 1 drop of each oil in palms and inhale deeply. Can be done every 1-2 hours if needed.

» Apply 2 drops Centering Blend or 2 drops Enlightening Blend to back of neck or bottom of the feet.

» Inhale Wintergreen or Rosemary directly from their bottles. Apply Tension Blend to palms of hands and deeply inhale.

» Diffuse Holiday Peaceful Blend and deeply inhale aroma.

Suggested Duration:

Use as needed in situations or feelings of betrayal. Use daily for 1 month if betrayal is fresh or has been held unprocessed in the body for a long time. Continue using any methods that support moving beyond feelings of betrayal.

Rigid

Oils and Blends:

Cassia, Eucalyptus, Cinnamon, Frankincense, Grapefruit, Green Mandarin, Lemon, Lavender, Vetiver, Ylang Ylang, Grounding Blend, Kid's Grounding Blend, Reassuring Blend, Restful Blend, Kid's Restful Blend

---

Additional Support:

Try applying Restful Blend or Kid's Restful Blend over heart and Grounding Blend or Kid's Grounding Blend on bottoms of feet. Sprinkle 3 drops each of Eucalyptus, Cassia, and Cinnamon onto cotton-wick inhaler and inhale deeply multiple times per day (refresh oils often). Or place 1 drop of each oil in palms and inhale deeply.

Testimony/Story:

"Sometimes I can get into moods where I am very rigid, unyielding, and needing things to go a certain way. ... Now, I use my inhaler with Eucalyptus, Cassia, and Cinnamon in it and it totally improves me for the better! I feel relaxed and open enough to consider other options without having a meltdown. ... I even diffuse it!" - Bondi W.

Protocol

» Apply Reassuring Blend over heart and deeply inhale.

» Apply Grounding Blend and Lavender to spine.

» Diffuse Ylang Ylang, Grapefruit, and Frankincense and inhale deeply for 5 breaths.

» Sprinkle 3 drops each of Lemon, Frankincense, and Green Mandarin onto cotton-wick inhaler and inhale deeply multiple times per day (refresh oils often). Or place 1 drop of each oil in palms and inhale deeply.

Suggested Duration:

Use daily as needed when feeling rigid, stubborn, or unyielding. Diffuse regularly in tense situations.

Sadness

Oils and Blends:

Grapefruit, Wild Orange, Lemon, Bergamot, Frankincense, Copaiba, Peppermint, Rosemary, Blue Tansy, Lemon, Inspiring Blend, Uplifting Blend, Invigorating Blend, Joyful Blend, Comforting Blend, Renewing Blend

Supplements:

Copaifera Softgels

Additional Support:

Try applying Comforting Blend and Renewing Blend over heart. Take 2 drops Frankincense or Copaiba under the tongue twice daily (or use Copaifera Softgels twice daily). Diffuse Uplifting Blend. Diffuse 2 drops Rosemary and 3 drops Frankincense.

Testimony/Story:

"Whenever I feel sad, I reach for my case of essential oils. The combination of Blue Tansy and Lemon reminds me of a blueberry muffin (with no calories!) and makes me smile every time. Citrus oils are also a sure-fire way to turn my frown upside-down. I just love my oils and rely on them for emotional support daily!" - Susan M.

Protocol

» Diffuse 2 drops each of Grapefruit, Wild Orange, Lemon, and Bergamot.[115]

» Apply 3 drops Blue Tansy and Lemon onto cotton-wick inhaler and carry with you inhaling deeply for 5 breaths multiple times per day (refresh oils often).[116]

» Apply Invigorating Blend and Joyful Blend over heart.

Suggested Duration:

Use for 1 month, then ongoing as needed to promote the processing of emotions and to uplift the mood.

Scarcity

Oils and Blends:

Blue Tansy, Wild Orange, Frankincense, Sandalwood, Lemon, Lavender, Eucalyptus, Peppermint, Tangerine, Anti-Aging Blend, Inspiring Blend, Invigorating Blend

---

Additional Support:

Try diffusing Invigorating Blend. Diffuse 3 drops each of Blue Tansy and Lemon. Apply Inspiring Blend over heart.

Protocol

» Diffuse Wild Orange, Frankincense, and Sandalwood.

» Diffuse Tangerine and Wild Orange.

» Apply Anti-Aging Blend over heart and deeply inhale for 5 breaths.

» Sprinkle 2 drops each of Lavender, Eucalypus, and Peppermint onto cotton-wick inhaler and inhale deeply multiple times per day (refresh oils often). Or place 1 drop of each oil in palms and inhale deeply.

Suggested Duration:

Use as long as needed to dispel scarcity mindset, and welcome the abundance of the universe. Continue to use any protocol that feels supportive to you on an ongoing basis.

Scattered

Oils and Blends:

Basil, Rosemary, Black Pepper, Peppermint, Lemon, Grapefruit, Frankincense, Geranium, Cardamom, Yarrow|Pom, Reassuring Blend, Focus Blend, Kid's Focus Blend, Restful Blend, Kid's Restful Blend, Captivating Blend

Supplements:

Energy & Stamina Complex

Additional Support:

Try diffusing 4 drops Frankincense, 2 drops Geranium, and 3 drops Cardamom. Diffuse 2 drops Peppermint, 2 drops Rosemary, and 3 drops Grapefruit in morning or during peak hours of needed focus and attention. Take 2 Energy & Stamina Complex in the morning. Apply Hopeful Blend in palms of hands, deeply inhale

Protocol

» Diffuse 4-5 drops of Reassuring Blend.

» Apply Focus Blend or Kid's Focus Blend to back of neck, massaging in thoroughly at base of hairline and into the brain stem. May also apply down spine for extra boost of focused energy.

» Apply Restful Blend over heart and deeply inhale.

» Sprinkle 2 drops each of Rosemary, Lemon, and Black Pepper onto cotton-wick inhaler and inhale deeply multiple times per day (refresh with oils every 5 days).[117]

» Inhale Basil directly from the bottle for 5 deep breaths.

» Apply Yarrow|Pom to palms and deeply inhale aroma.

Suggested Duration:

Use ongoing daily as needed. These protocols are wonderfully supportive and can be used ongoing for however long is needed.

Schizophrenia/Schizoaffective Disorder

Oils and Blends:

Blue Tansy, Bergamot, Copaiba, Eucalyptus, Frankincense, Grapefruit, Helichrysum, Lavender, Lemon, Melissa, Peppermint, Roman Chamomile, Rose, Rosemary, Basil, Spearmint, Spikenard, Vetiver, Wild Orange, Ylang Ylang, Steadying Blend, Restful Blend, Reassuring Blend

Supplements:

Copaifera Softgels

Additional Support:

Try diffusing 2 drops Clove Bud, 6 drops Grapefruit, 2 drops Roman Chamomile. Inhale Basil directly from the bottle. Sprinkle 1 drop Geranium, 1 drop Melissa, 1 drop Ylang Ylang, and 3 drops Frankincense onto cotton-wick inhaler and inhale deeply multiple times per day (refresh oils often).

Testimony/Story:

"Restful Blend and Reassuring Blend have been an absolute godsend in our home for my son who is Schizoaffective. He becomes so worked up, anxious, sad, delusional, and paranoid all at once that some days there is nothing I can do other than turn on a diffuser nearby him or rub the back of his neck with a few drops of oil. Before the oils, his episodes would last for DAYS or WEEKS, and it was miserable for the whole family. Now, the episodes last only 15-30 minutes and sometimes even disappear immediately. He gets distracted by the aroma and it changes the story feedback loop in his brain so he can focus on something different. I cannot say enough good things about these oils--we use these two and many more with him now!" - Mae M.

Protocol:

» Apply 2 drops Frankincense or Copaiba under the tongue twice daily and/or use 1-2 Copaifera Softgels twice daily.

» Apply 3 drops Blue Tansy and Lemon onto cotton-wick inhaler and inhale deeply multiple times per day (refresh with oils every 5 days).[118] Or place 1 drop of each oil in palms and inhale deeply. Can be done every 1-2 hours if needed.

» Take Restful Blend Softgels 30 min before bedtime and diffuse 2 drops Spikenard with 3 drops Vetiver next to bed (you can also apply these oils to the bottom of your feet).[119]

» Diffuse 2 drops each of Grapefruit, Wild Orange, Lemon, and Bergamot when feeling irritable or depressed.

With Paranoia/Delusions:

» Diffuse Steadying Blend or Restful Blend.

» Apply 3 drops Vetiver or Reassuring Blend over heart and deeply inhale for 5-6 breaths.

» Diffuse 2 drops each of Spearmint, Wild Orange, and Peppermint.

» Apply 3 drops Lemon, 2 drops Rose, and 3 drops Eucalyptus to cotton-wick inhaler and inhale deeply multiple times per day (refresh oils often). Or place 1 drop of each oil in palms and inhale deeply.

» Sprinkle 2 drops each of Ylang Ylang, Spikenard, and Helichrysum onto cotton-wick inhaler and inhale deeply multiple times per day (refresh oils often). Or place 1 drop of each oil in palms and inhale deeply.[120]

» Put 1 drop of Melissa oil on thumb and press it to the roof of the mouth, holding for 15 seconds.[121]

Suggested Duration:

Use daily as a stabilizing practice on an ongoing basis.

Self Doubt

Oils and Blends:

Bergamot, Geranium, Patchouli, Bergamot, Jasmine, Ylang Ylang, Sandalwood, Lemon, Litsea, Peppermint, Rosemary, Eucalyptus, Rose, Thyme, Cedarwood, Juniper Berry, Fennel, Thyme, Grounding Blend, Blend for Women, Monthly Blend, Courage Blend, Hopeful Blend

---

Additional Support:

Try applying Courage Blend into palms of hands and deeply inhaling for 5 breaths. Women may choose to use Courage Blend or try the Blend for Women over the heart and back of neck. Diffuse 1 drop Ylang Ylang, 1 drops Jasmine, and 2 drops Bergamot. Apply Hopeful Blend to palms of hands and deeply inhale for 5 breaths.

Protocol

» Apply 1 drop each Geranium, Jasmine, and Sandalwood to neck and shoulders and massage into skin with some fractionated coconut oil.

» Apply Grounding Blend to bottom of the feet and over heart.

» Apply 3 drops Lemon, 2 drops Rose, and 3 drops Eucalyptus to cotton-wick inhaler and inhale deeply multiple times per day (refresh oils often).

» Diffuse 1 drop Cedarwood, 2 drops Juniper Berry, and 1 drop Thyme.

» Diffuse 2 drops Peppermint, 1 drop Fennel, 1 drop Litsea, and 1 drop Rosemary.

Suggested Duration:

Use daily for 2 months. Continue to use any methods above that support feelings of self confidence ongoing for as long as needed.

Self-Righteous

Oils and Blends:

Cassia, Eucalyptus, Cinnamon, Frankincense, Grapefruit, Green Mandarin, Lemon, Vetiver, Ylang Ylang, Grounding Blend, Kid's Grounding Blend, Reassuring Blend, Renewing Blend, Restful Blend, Kid's Restful Blend

---

Additional Support:

Try applying Restful Blend or Kid's Restful Blend over heart and Grounding Blend or Kid's Grounding Blend on bottom of the feet. Sprinkle 3 drops each of Eucalyptus, Cassia, and Cinnamon onto cotton-wick inhaler and inhale deeply multiple times per day (refresh oils often). Or place 1 drop of each oil in palms and inhale deeply.

Protocol

» Apply Reassuring Blend or Renewing Blend over heart and deeply inhale for 5 breaths.

» Diffuse Ylang Ylang, Grapefruit, and Frankincense and inhale deeply for 5 breaths.

» Sprinkle 3 drops each of Lemon, Frankincense, and Green Mandarin onto cotton-wick inhaler and inhale deeply multiple times per day (refresh oils often). Or place 1 drop of each oil in palms and inhale deeply.

Suggested Duration:

Use daily as needed when feeling prideful. Diffuse regularly in tense situations.

Separation Anxiety Disorder

Oils and Blends:

Bergamot, Wild Orange, Cypress, Frankincense, Lavender, Lemon, Lime, Grapefruit, Tangerine, Roman Chamomile, Rose, Reassuring Blend, Restful Blend, Grounding Blend, Invigorating Blend, Joyful Blend

Additional Support:

If you're not yet seeing the results you'd like to see, try diffusing Invigorating Blend. Apply Rose over heart. Research shows that citrus oils are a wonderful aid in reducing feelings of anxiety. Sprinkle 2 drops each of Grapefruit, Wild Orange, Lemon, and Bergamot onto cotton-wick inhaler and inhale deeply multiple times per day (refresh oils often). Or diffuse 2 drops of each oil together.

Testimony/Story:

"My daughter has had really bad separation anxiety with me since she was about 7 or so. When I dropped her off at school she would cry and hold onto my leg refusing to let me go, and telling me she was afraid I'd die in a car accident. We started applying Reassuring Blend to her spine before bed and I'd spend some extra time with her then. I also made her a special inhaler with a few of her favorite oils in it. Now when I drop her off we use Reassuring Blend together before she gets out of the car and I send her with her favorite oils in an inhaler to use when she gets nervous. She feels comfortable and stays at school or church with no problems and I'm so glad to see her happy again!" - Renea C.

Protocol

» Apply 1-2 drops Reassuring Blend to palms of hands and deeply inhale for 5 breaths.[122]

» Apply 1-2 drops Restful Blend over heart and on the back of the neck.[123]

» Apply 2-3 drops Grounding Blend to wrists and bottom of the feet.

» Sprinkle 2 drops Frankincense, 2 drops Bergamot, and 4 drops Wild Orange onto cotton-wick inhaler and inhale deeply multiple times per day (refresh oils often).[124] Or place 1 drop of each oil in palms and inhale deeply.

» Diffuse 2 drops each of Cypress, Lavender, Frankincense, and Roman Chamomile throughout the day.

Suggested Duration:

Use ongoing during periods of separation caused anxiety. Use one or more of the protocols as needed to support a calm emotional state, and to achieve the results that feel best in your body.

Shame

Oils and Blends:

Bergamot, Copaiba, Ylang Ylang, Wild Orange, Black Pepper, Peppermint, Comforting Blend, Renewing Blend, Reassuring Blend, Respiratory Blend, Holiday Peaceful Blend

Supplements:

Fruit and Veggie Drink, Copaifera Softgels

Additional Support:

Try inhaling Black Pepper directly from the bottle for 5 deep breaths. Diffuse Respiratory Blend. Mix 1 drop Peppermint with 12 oz of water and drink. Guilt can have a detrimental effect on one's health so adding in 1 scoop of Fruit and Veggie drink in the morning can help support getting key nutrients and antioxidants and reduce cellular damage done by feeling shame.

Protocol

» Apply Comforting Blend and Renewing Blend over the heart and take 4-5 deep breaths.

» Diffuse Reassuring Blend or Holiday Peaceful Blend and deeply inhale aroma.

» Sprinkle 2 drops Bergamot, 1 drop Ylang Ylang, and 3 drops Wild Orange onto cotton-wick inhaler and inhale deeply multiple times per day (refresh oils often). Or place 1 drop of each oil in palms and inhale deeply.

» Take 1-2 Copaifera Softgels twice daily.

Suggested Duration:

Use for 3 weeks minimum. Use ongoing as needed for support.

Shock

Oils and Blends:

Frankincense, Roman Chamomile, Rose, Lavender, Lemon, Geranium, Douglas Fir, Ginger, Vetiver, Cedarwood, Jasmine, Comforting Blend

Supplements:

Restful Complex Softgels, Digestive Enzymes, Digestive Tabs

Additional Support:

Try adding Digestive Enzymes or Digest Tablets with meals to support healthy digestion. The digestive process and sleep patterns are frequently disturbed when in shock and by adding additional support they can prove beneficial. Apply 2 drops Jasmine and 1 drop Cedarwood to stomach before bed. Take 1-3 Restful Complex Softgels prior to bed or before napping.

Protocol

» Diffuse 1 drop Roman Chamomile, 2 drops Douglas Fir, 1 drop Geranium, and 2 drops Frankincense.

» Drink 8+ oz water with 1 drop lemon oil in it.

» Apply 2 drops each of Ginger, Geranium, and Lemon on to cotton-wick inhaler and inhale deeply for 5 breaths multiple times a day as needed.

» Apply 2 drops each Rose and Vetiver and massage into neck and shoulders with fractionated coconut oil prior to sleeping or napping.

Suggested Duration:

Use daily as needed for two weeks minimum. Continue to use as needed to support calming and balancing central nervous system.

Social Anxiety

Oils and Blends:

Bergamot, Wild Orange, Douglas Fir, Frankincense, Lavender, Lemon, Lime, Grapefruit, Tangerine, Roman Chamomile, Rose, Vetiver, Reassuring Blend, Restful Blend, Grounding Blend, Soothing Blend.

Additional Support:

Try sprinkling 2 drops each of Grapefruit, Wild Orange, Lemon, and Bergamot onto cotton-wick inhaler and inhale deeply multiple times per day (refresh oils often). Or diffuse 2 drops of each oil together. Also see Insecurity protocol. Apply Soothing Blend to neck and shoulders to relieve emotional tension.

Testimony/Story:

"Big crowds and groups of people are my mortal enemy. I cannot stand to socialize with strangers or to be in big groups of people I don't know or barely know. I started using an inhaler with Douglas Fir, Frankincense, and Roman Chamomile in it. I cannot explain HOW it works but when I use it before going into social situations I feel grounded, free, and spacious instead of crowded and claustrophobic. It's made going to work functions, social gatherings, and shopping malls heaps easier for me." - Rachel K.

Protocol

» Apply 1-2 drops Restful Blend over heart and deeply inhale for 5 breaths.[125]

» Apply 1-2 drops Reassuring Blend to palms of hands and deeply inhale for 5 breaths.[126]

» Apply 2-3 drops Grounding Blend to back of neck and wrists.

» Sprinkle 2 drops Douglas Fir, 2 drops Frankincense, and 2 drops Roman Chamomile onto cotton-wick inhaler and inhale deeply multiple times per day (refresh oils often). Or place 1 drop of each oil in hands and inhale deeply.

» Diffuse 3 drops each of Lemon and Lavender.[127]

Suggested Duration:

Use anytime social anxiety is present and continue to use regularly until feelings of anxiety begin to lessen and eventually dissipate altogether. Continue to use any protocol that feels supportive to the body.

Stress

Oils and Blends:

Birch, Ylang Ylang, Roman Chamomile, Lavender, Tangerine, Wild Orange, Lemon, Grapefruit, Vetiver, Copaiba, Frankincense, Cedarwood, Sandalwood, Spikenard, Holiday Peaceful Blend, Reassuring Blend, Restful Blend, Grounding Blend, Kid's Restful Blend, Kid's Grounding Blend, Tension Blend

Supplements:

Restful Complex Softgels, Copaifera Softgels

Additional Support:

Try diffusing 6-7 drops Frankincense. Diffuse 2 drops each of Grapefruit, Wild Orange, Lemon, and Tangerine. Diffuse Holiday Peaceful Blend. Apply Cedarwood to bottoms of feet and Sandalwood down the spine and back of the neck. Take Restful Complex Softgels 30 min prior to sleep if feeling overstimulated before bedtime and inhale Restful Blend from bottle with 5-6 breaths before laying down to sleep. Inhale Birch or Tension Blend from bottle. Apply Tension Blend on back of neck. Also see Insomnia protocol.

Testimony/Story:

"My mother had fallen terminally ill and there was so much stress in our lives from managing her medical care, navigating her end of life estate issues, and dealing with family members who were not supportive or handling it well. If I hadn't had Copaifera Softgels, Cedarwood, and my citrus oils, I think I would have gone mad or just curled up in a ball in a corner. Using my oils everyday took the edge off enough so I could function and get what I needed to get done that day. It was still hard, but it was doable with my oils."
- Deanna D.

Protocol

» Diffuse Restful Blend nearby and inhale deeply as it diffuses.[128]

» Apply Reassuring Blend over heart and take 5 deep breaths.[129]

» Take 2 Copaifera Softgels twice daily.

» Sprinkle 2 drops each of Frankincense, Roman Chamomile, and Lavender onto cotton-wick inhaler and inhale deeply multiple times per day (refresh oils often). Or place 1 drop of each oil in palms and inhale deeply.

» For Kids: Apply Reassuring Blend over heart, Kid's Restful Blend to back of neck, and Kid's Grounding Blend to feet. Diffuse Reassuring Blend.

Suggested Duration:

Use daily as needed for feelings of stress. Continue any methods ongoing that work well as a daily protocol to help dissipate energy and prevent stress.

Stuck

Oils and Blends:

Cypress, Eucalyptus, Frankincense, Cilantro, Coriander, Patchouli, Juniper Berry, Clary Sage, Litsea, Bergamot, Wild Orange, Ginger, Cedarwood, Thyme, Turmeric, Lemongrass, Rosemary, Encouraging Blend

Supplements:

Detoxification Softgels

Additional Support:

Try exchanging Juniper Berry in above inhaler protocol for either Ginger, Thyme, Coriander, or Cedarwood. Diffuse 2 drops Lemongrass, 2 drops each of Wild Orange, Bergamot, and Rosemary. Inhale Litsea directly from the bottle. Take 1-2 Detoxification Softgels twice daily to promote clearing and cleansing internally to get energy moving. Inhale Cilantro from the bottle.

Protocol

» Apply 2 drops each of Cypress, Eucalyptus, Frankincense, and Juniper Berry onto cotton-wick inhaler (refresh inhaler with new oils every 3-7 days).

» Diffuse 2 drops each of Wild Orange, Bergamot, & Rosemary.

» Apply Encouraging Blend over heart.

» Apply 1 drop Patchouli to Aromatherapy inhaler or jewelry and smell it often.

» Take 1 drop of Turmeric oil internally in vegetable capsule twice daily with meals.

Suggested Duration:

Use protocol for two weeks consecutively. Continue using any of the above methods that feel supportive to you ongoing as needed.

Suicidal

Oils and Blends:

Basil, Bergamot, Cinnamon, Coriander, Copaiba, Eucalyptus, Frankincense, Jasmine, Lavender, Magnolia, Marjoram, Melissa, Peppermint, Rose, Rosemary, Tangerine, Ylang Ylang, Joyful Blend, Invigorating Blend, Comforting Blend, Renewing Blend

Supplements:

Copaifera Softgels

Additional Support:

Try diffusing Comforting Blend or Renewing Blend. May also feel relief by applying Comforting Blend or Renewing Blend over heart and deeply inhaling for 5 breaths. Diffuse 3 drops Tangerine, 2 drops Ylang Ylang, 2 drops Bergamot. Apply Magnolia on back of neck and wrists. Apply Jasmine over heart and down spine.

Protocol

» 2 drops Frankincense or Copaiba under the tongue twice daily and/or use 1-2 Copaifera Softgels twice daily.

» Apply 1 drop of Melissa oil to the thumb and press to the roof of your mouth, holding for 15 seconds.[130]

» Apply Rose over heart and deeply inhale for 5 breaths.

» Apply Lavender to bottom of the feet.

» Diffuse 2 drops each of Eucalyptus, Coriander, and Peppermint to lift the fog of depression.[131]

» Diffuse 2 drops each Cinnamon, Basil, & Rosemary to strengthen a weak will.

Suggested Duration:

Use daily for 3 months minimum. Continue to use protocols as needed to support a balanced and healthy mood state.

Trauma

Oils and Blends:

Basil, Pink Pepper, Cedarwood, Copaiba, Clary Sage, Eucalyptus, Fennel, Frankincense, Helichrysum, Jasmine, Juniper Berry, Lavender, Rosemary, Lemon, Lime, Magnolia, Melissa, Neroli, Patchouli, Roman Chamomile, Rose, Turmeric, Spearmint, Spikenard, Wild Orange, Ylang Ylang, Comforting Blend, Restful Blend, Joyful Blend

Supplements:

Restful Complex Softgels, Copaifera Softgels

Additional Support:

Try adding 1 drop Melissa oil to thumb and press to roof of mouth, holding for 30 seconds. Try sprinkling 2 drops each of Ylang Ylang, Spikenard, and Helichrysum onto cotton-wick inhaler and inhale deeply multiple times per day (refresh oils often). Or place 1 drop of each oil in palms and inhale deeply. Diffuse 2 drops Rosemary and 3 drops Juniper Berry to inhale during therapy sessions. Apply 2 drops each of Juniper Berry, Rosemary, and Patchouli onto cotton-wick inhaler and inhale deeply multiple times per day (refresh oils often). This aromatherapy inhaler blend may be useful to use while in therapy sessions or while journaling and reprocessing an event. Apply Joyful Blend over the heart. Take 1-3 capsules Restful Complex Softgels 30 min before bed.

Protocol

» Alternate diffusing 4-6 drops Restful Blend then 5-6 drops Frankincense in diffuser throughout the day and place diffuser in close proximity to you.

» Apply Comforting Blend or Restful Blend over the heart and deeply inhale aroma for 5 breaths.

» Take 2 drops Frankincense under tongue and 2 capsules Copaifera Softgels twice daily.

» Take 1 drop of Turmeric oil internally in vegetable capsule twice daily with meals.

» Sprinkle 2 drops each of Clary Sage, Roman Chamomile, and Pink Pepper onto cotton-wick inhaler and inhale deeply multiple times per day (refresh oils often). Or place 1 drop of each oil in palms and inhale deeply.

» Apply Jasmine, Magnolia, and Neroli to the spine or apply to the back of the neck or bottom of the feet.[132]

» Diffuse 2 drops each of Wild Orange, Lime, and Spearmint.

Suggested Duration:

Use daily for 3 months. Continue to use ongoing as needed to support a relaxed emotional state.

Tourette Syndrome

Oils and Blends:

Clove Bud, Coriander, Copaiba, Cinnamon, Cardamom, Lemon, Grapefruit, Roman Chamomile, Sandalwood, Basil, Frankincense, Grounding Blend, Patchouli, Wild Orange, Uplifting Blend, Cellular Complex Blend, Restful Blend, Kid's Restful Blend

Supplements:

Cellular Complex Softgel, Copaifera Softgel, Restful Complex Softgel

---

Additional Support:

Try diffusing 2 drops Coriander, 2 drops Basil, and 2 drops Lemon for a mentally energizing aroma. Diffuse Uplifting Blend for cheery mood support. Diffuse 2 drops Cinnamon, 3 drops Wild Orange and 3 drops Cardamom for a neuroprotective, uplifting blend. Take Restful Complex Softgels 30 min prior to bed.

Protocol

» Apply Restful Blend or Kid's Restful Blend on back of neck to relax and ease anxiety.

» Diffuse 2 drops Clove Bud, 6 drops Grapefruit, and 2 drops Roman Chamomile for relaxing, uplifting, and neuroprotective properties of blend.[133]

» Take 2 Cellular Complex Softgels twice daily for brain support.

» Take 2 drops Frankincense or Copaiba under the tongue twice daily and/or use 1-2 Copaifera Softgels twice daily.

» Massage 2 drops each of Frankincense and Sandalwood onto parts of the body that experience tics or involuntary movement.

» Apply Grounding Blend or Restful Blend to bottom of the feet and over heart.

Suggested Duration:

Use daily for neuroprotective support, uplifting the mood, and relaxing the nervous system.

Unforgiving

Oils and Blends:

Eucalyptus, Frankincense, Geranium, Green Mandarin, Lemon, Vetiver, Ylang Ylang, Grounding Blend, Kid's Grounding Blend, Reassuring Blend, Comforting Blend, Renewing Blend, Restful Blend, Kid's Restful Blend

---

Additional Support:

Try applying Restful Blend or Kid's Restful Blend over heart and Grounding Blend or Kid's Grounding Blend on bottoms of feet. Apply Reassuring Blend over heart. Sprinkle 3 drops each of Eucalyptus, Cassia, and Cinnamon onto cotton-wick inhaler and inhale deeply multiple times per day (refresh oils often). Or place 1 drop of each oil into diffuser.

Protocol

» Apply Grounding Blend or Kid's Grounding Blend to bottom of the feet.

» Apply Restful Blend or Kid's Restful Blend over heart and deeply inhale for 5 breaths.

» Diffuse Steadying Blend and deeply inhale for 5 breaths.

» Sprinkle 3 drops each of Lemon, Lavender, and Siberian Fir onto cotton-wick inhaler and inhale deeply multiple times per day (refresh oils often). Or place 1 drop of each oil in palms and inhale deeply.

Suggested Duration:

Use daily as needed when feeling rigid, stubborn, or unyielding. Diffuse regularly in tense situations.

Unstable

Oils and Blends:

Arborvitae, Douglas Fir, Siberian Fir, Eucalyptus, Lavender, Lemon, Frankincense, Grapefruit, Spearmint, Grounding Blend, Kid's Grounding Blend, Restful Blend, Kid's Restful Blend, Steadying Blend, Holiday Joyful Blend

Supplements:

Vitality Trio Complex

Additional Support:

Try diffusing 2 drops each of Frankincense, Grapefruit, and Douglas Fir. Diffuse Holiday Joyful Blend. Diffuse 2 drops Arborvitae and 3 drops Spearmint. Omega's found in the Vitality Trio Complex will be helpful to stabilize brain health.

Protocol

» Apply Grounding Blend or Kid's Grounding Blend to bottom of the feet.

» Apply Restful Blend or Kid's Restful Blend over heart and deeply inhale for 5 breaths.

» Diffuse Steadying Blend and deeply inhale for 5 breaths.

» Sprinkle 3 drops each of Lemon, Lavender, and Siberian Fir onto cotton-wick inhaler and inhale deeply multiple times per day (refresh oils often). Or place 1 drop of each oil in palms and inhale deeply.

Suggested Duration:

Use daily for a week to help stabilize and ground into a more healthy emotional state. Continue to use any protocol that supports you to feel emotionally balanced.

Upheaval

Oils and Blends:

Douglas Fir, Siberian Fir, Eucalyptus, Lavender, Lemon, Frankincense, Grapefruit, Grounding Blend, Kid's Grounding Blend, Restful Blend, Kid's Restful Blend, Enlightening Blend, Steadying Blend, Comforting Blend, Renewing Blend

Supplements:

Vitality Trio Complex

Additional Support:

Try applying Restful Blend or Kid's Restful Blend over heart and deeply inhale for 5 breaths. Diffuse 2 drops each Frankincense, Grapefruit, and Douglas Fir. Alternate applying Comforting Blend then Renewing Blend over heart. Omega's found in the Vitality Trio Complex help the brain when there is a lot of change going on.

Protocol

» Apply Grounding Blend or Kid's Grounding Blend to bottom of the feet.

» Apply Steadying Blend on back of neck and deeply inhale residual aroma left on hands for 5 breaths.

» Diffuse Enlightening Blend and deeply inhale for 5 breaths.

» Sprinkle 3 drops each of Lemon, Lavender, and Siberian Fir onto cotton-wick inhaler and inhale deeply multiple times per day (refresh oils often). Or place 1 drop of each oil in palms and inhale deeply.

Suggested Duration:

Use daily to help stabilize and ground into a more healthy emotional state for a week. Continue to use any protocol that supports you feeling emotionally balanced.

Weak-Willed

Oils and Blends:

Bergamot, Birch, Grapefruit, Cinnamon, Basil, Rosemary, Lemongrass, Ginger, Mānuka, Digestive Blend, Protective Blend, Grounding Blend

---

Additional Support:

Try diffusing Protective Blend. Diffuse 2 drops each of Ginger, Grapefruit, and Lemon. Diffuse Birch or inhale directly from bottle. Apply Mānuka to the wrists.

Protocol

» Diffuse 2 drops each of Cinnamon, Basil, and Rosemary.

» Sprinkle 3 drops each of Lemongrass, Bergamot, and Grapefruit onto cotton-wick inhaler and inhale deeply multiple times per day (refresh oils often). Or place 1 drop of each oil in palms and inhale deeply.

» Apply Digestive Blend around navel.

» Apply Grounding Blend to bottom of the feet.

Suggested Duration:

Use daily to strengthen internal will and sense of determination. Use daily as long as needed to accomplish overcoming obstacles.

Willful (Excessive)

Oils and Blends:

Copaiba, Grapefruit, Wild Orange, Lemon, Lavender, Bergamot, Frankincense, Vetiver, Focus Blend, Kid's Focus Blend, Reassuring Blend, Restful Blend, Kid's Restful Blend

Supplements:

Copaifera Softgels

Additional Support:

Try adding 1-2 Copaifera Softgels twice daily. Diffuse 6-7 drops Frankincense and apply oil down spine and back of neck. Apply 2 drops Vetiver over heart or diffuse 3 drops each Vetiver and Frankincense.

Protocol

» Apply Reassuring Blend, Restful Blend, or Kid's Restful Blend over heart. May choose to cycle through these three oils, applying over the heart throughout the day or use a different oil depending on the day.

» Diffuse 2 drops each of Grapefruit, Wild Orange, Lemon, and Bergamot to promote calming, uplifting energy in the environment.

» Sprinkle 4 drops Frankincense, 3 drops Wild Orange, and 2 drops Lavender onto Aromatherapy inhaler or jewelry and inhale often.

» Apply Kid's Focus Blend to back of neck to focus attention in a positive manner.

Suggested Duration:

Use daily as a preventative measure to help keep interactions pleasant and peaceful. Choose one or two protocols as interventions to use when excessively willful behavior occurs.

Workaholism

Oils and Blends:

Ylang Ylang, Roman Chamomile, Lavender, Tangerine, Wild Orange, Lemon, Grapefruit, Vetiver, Copaiba, Frankincense, Cedarwood, Sandalwood, Spikenard, Reassuring Blend, Restful Blend, Grounding Blend, Kid's Restful Blend, Kid's Grounding Blend

Supplements:

Restful Complex Softgels, Copaifera Softgels

Additional Support:

Try diffusing 6-7 drops Frankincense. Diffuse 2 drops each of Grapefruit, Wild Orange, Lemon, and Tangerine. Apply Cedarwood to bottoms of feet and Sandalwood down the spine and back of the neck. Take Restful Complex Softgels 30 min prior to sleep if feeling overstimulated before bedtime and inhale Restful Blend from bottle with 5-6 breaths before laying down to sleep. Also see Insomnia protocol.

Testimony/Story:

"I used to believe that the harder I worked the more successful I could become. Instead, I realized that the harder I worked, people would be happy to put more on my plate and that it didn't necessarily lead to success. Also, the more I worked, the less I saw my family and that strained our relationships. I knew all of this logically, but have struggled to stop working as much as I feel this compulsion to keep grinding away for success. To help me get my priorities straight, I diffuse oils first thing in the morning to set the tone for my mood, and also carry an inhaler with Frankincense, Roman Chamomile, and Lavender in it to help me relax and reset when I notice myself going into 'grind mode' or overcommitting my work schedule again. I am finally beginning to feel peaceful around my worklife." - Carl H.

Protocol

» Diffuse Restful Blend nearby and inhale deeply for 5 breaths as it diffuses.

» Apply Reassuring Blend over heart and take 5 deep breaths.

» Take 2 Copaifera Softgels twice daily.

» Sprinkle 2 drops each of Frankincense, Roman Chamomile, and Lavender onto Aromatherapy inhaler or jewelry and smell multiple times a day (refresh oils often).

» **For Kids:** Apply Reassuring Blend over heart, Kid's Restful Blend to back of neck, and Kid's Grounding Blend to feet. Diffuse Reassuring Blend.

» **For Women:** Inhale Magnolia from the bottle or apply it to wrists/neck as perfume.

» **For Men:** Inhale InTune from the bottle or apply it to wrists/neck as cologne.

Suggested Duration:

Use daily as needed for feelings of stress. Continue any methods that work well as a daily ongoing protocol to help dissipate energy and prevent stress.

Worry

Oils and Blends:

Cassia, Cilantro, Cedarwood, Cinnamon, Frankincense, Geranium, Grapefruit, Juniper Berry, Lavender, Magnolia, Marjoram, Melissa, Neroli, Peppermint, Roman Chamomile, Rose, Spearmint, Vetiver, Wild Orange, Reassuring Blend, Restful Blend, Kid's Restful Blend, Grounding Blend, Kid's Grounding Blend

Additional Support:

Try applying Cedarwood to bottom of the feet. Diffuse 2 drops each of Cassia and Spearmint. Place 1 drop each of Peppermint and Neroli in palms of hands and deeply inhale for 5 deep breaths. Diffuse 3 drops Vetiver and 2 drops Roman Chamomile. Inhale Cinnamon or Cilantro directly from the bottle. Apply Magnolia to wrists and back of neck. Apply 3 drops Melissa, 2 drops Marjoram, and 2 drops Geranium onto cotton-wick inhaler and inhale deeply multiple times per day (refresh oils often). Or place 1 drop of each oil in palms and inhale deeply. Can be done every 1-2 hours if needed.

Testimony/Story:

"My husband works as a police officer and I sometimes struggle with a lot of feelings of worry and concern when he's away on the job. My worry used to negatively impact my sleep, my friendships, and my marriage. Now, whenever I feel worried, I reach for my oils. The woodsy/earthy oils and citrus oils are my favorite for making me feel calm. Now I can help calm my worrying-heart and mind and I noticed that it does not consume my days and nights like it used to. I am able to feel peaceful." - Amanda S.

Protocol

» Apply Reassuring Blend over heart and deeply inhale for 5 breaths.

» Apply Restful Blend over heart and Grounding Blend on bottom of the feet.

» Sprinkle 2 drops each of Frankincense, Roman Chamomile, and Lavender onto cotton-wick inhaler and inhale deeply multiple times per day (refresh oils often). Or place 1 drop of each oil in palms and inhale deeply.

» Sprinkle 3 drops Grapefruit, 3 drops Lemon, and 2 drops Geranium onto cotton-wick inhaler and inhale deeply multiple times per day (refresh oils often). Or place 1 drop of each oil in palms and inhale deeply.

» For Kids: Apply Kid's Grounding Blend on bottoms of feet and Kid's Restful Blend over heart. Diffuse Reassuring Blend or 3 drops Lavender and 3 drops Frankincense.

Suggested Duration:

Use daily as needed to support healthy mood state.

Section 2

How to Use Essential Oils & Oil Blends (A-Z)

Arborvitae

Use to Support These Positive Emotions and Experiences:
Confidence, Clarity, Gumption, Relaxed, Strength, Stability,
Supports the Brain

Use to Balance These Negative Emotions and Experiences:
Body Dysmorphia, Confusion, Feelings of Instability, Negative
Family Patterns

Did you know? Arborvitae is a powerful expectorant as well.
It is great to use topically on the chest when sick with a cough,
as it powerfully clears out the lungs and relaxes the body. It is
also a wonderful neuroprotectant.[1]

Experience Arborvitae: Apply 1 drop to the palm of your
hand, or inhale directly from the bottle, to experience the
woodsy, soothing aroma of this essential oil.

Basil

Use to Support These Positive Emotions and Experiences:
Boldness, Confidence, Clarity, Determination, Energized, Focus,
Reduce Mental Fatigue, Relaxed, Sedating, Self Acceptance,
Strengthen Will

Use to Balance These Negative Emotions and Experiences:
Bipolar Disorder, Body Dysmorphia, Codependency,
Confusion, Delusions, Envy, Fear, Gender Dysphoria, Hate,
Impatience, Jealousy, Limit Beliefs, Listlessness, Negative
Family Patterns, Parasitic Relationships, Panic Disorder,
Paranoia, Parkinson's Disease, Phobias, Psychosis, Trauma,
Lack of Purpose, Schizophrenia, Trauma, Tourette Syndrome

Did you know? Basil's high level of Linalool helps to create a
relaxing experience for users and it's contents of Eucalyptol
can create a refreshing experience immediately upon
inhalation. It helps to prevent mental fatigue and burnout.[2]

Experience Basil: Inhale Basil directly from the bottle to re-
energize your mental state and relax your body at the same
time.

Bergamot

Use to Support These Positive Emotions and Experiences:
Confidence, Encouraged, Fulfillment, Levity, Peacefulness, Patience, Positivity, Trust

Use to Balance These Negative Emotions and Experiences:
Addiction, Anger, Annoyed, Anxiety, Autism/Aspergers, Betrayal, Bipolar, Bulimia, Codependency, Conduct Disorder, Oppositional Defiant Disorder, Critical, Debilitated, Depression, Despair, Envy, Embarrassed, Emptiness, Fear, Frustrated, Gender Dysphoria, Guilt, Impatience, Jealousy, Lack of Boundaries, Limiting Belief, Overeating, Parasitic Relationships, Perfectionism, Rage, Regret, Rejection, Sadness, Schizophrenia, Schizoaffective Disorder, Self Doubt, Separation Anxiety Disorder, Shame, Suicidal, Weak Willed

Did you know? Bergamot's high level of Limonene is what makes it great for relieving stress, elevating mood, and helps to increase absorption of other terpenes, which is why Bergamot is often included in many blends.[3]

Experience Bergamot: Diffuse 3 drops Bergamot to uplift your mood.

Birch

Use to Support These Positive Emotions and Experiences:
Positive, Stimulating, Supported, Uplifting

Use to Balance These Negative Emotions and Experiences:
Bitterness, Critical, Fatigue, Holding onto Past, Isolated, Purposeless, Stress, Weak Willed

Did you know? Birch has a minty-fresh aroma similar to wintergreen oil.

Experience Birch: Inhale Birch directly from bottle to feel a burst of minty energy.

Black Pepper

Use to Support These Positive Emotions and Experiences:
Breaks Cycles of Addiction, Confidence, Focus, Forgiveness, Integrity, Self Assurance

Use to Balance These Negative Emotions and Experiences:
Addiction, ADD/ADHD, Anorexia, Betrayal, Embarrassed, Guilt, Regret, Rejection, Scattered, Shame

Did you know? The amount of b-pinene in Black Pepper means this oil has antidepressant properties. According to multiple studies, it is an ideal oil to use while quitting smoking as it has a history of success in helping individuals quit.[4]

Experience Black Pepper: Inhale Black Pepper directly from bottle to experience the bold, peppery aroma and give your mood a boost.

Blue Tansy

Use to Support These Positive Emotions and Experiences:
Abundance, Clarity, Confidence, Energy, Excitement, Inner Peace, Patience, Relaxed, Self Assurance

Use to Balance These Negative Emotions and Experiences:
Apathy, Bipolar Disorder, Controlling, Critical, Depression, Frustrated, Gender Dysphoria, Impatient, Listless/Lost, Negative Family Patterns, Obsessive Compulsive Behavior, Panic, Purposeless, Resignation, Sadness, Scarcity, Schizophrenia

Did you know? Anecdotally, Blue Tansy is known in some circles as the oil of "making it happen" and getting through mental blocks. Apply 1 drop of Blue Tansy to your big toe twice daily for 30 days and see for yourself what transpires in your life!

Experience Blue Tansy: Inhale directly from the bottle to experience a sweet, relaxing, floral aromatic note that puts you immediately at ease.

Cardamom

Use to Support These Positive Emotions and Experiences:
Focus, Patience, Peacefulness, Self Assurance

Use to Balance These Negative Emotions and Experiences:
ADD/ADHD, Alzheimers, Blame, Codependency, Controlling, Lack of Boundaries, Parasitic Relationships, Parkinson's Disease, Scattered, Tourette Syndrome

Did you know? Cardamom has a high level of Esters, which make this oil ideal for relaxation. Use this before bed if you are anxious and have trouble sleeping.

Experience Cardamom: Diffuse Cardamom to inspire feelings of peacefulness and patience.

Cassia

Use to Support These Positive Emotions and Experiences:
Brave, Confidence, Forgiveness, Peacefulness, Relaxed, Seeing From Another's Perspective

Use to Balance These Negative Emotions and Experiences:
Anxiety, Embarrassed, Have to be Right, Pride, Rigid, Self-Righteous, Unforgiving, Workaholism, Worry

Did you know? Cassia is frequently used in place of Cinnamon Bark in cooking and flavoring due to it's similar aroma and flavor profile, and at a more affordable price. Both oils have high levels of aldehydes in them which causes a simultaneously uplifting and calming effect when inhaled.[5]

Experience Cassia: Inhale Cassia directly from the bottle or diffuse 2 drops in a diffuser to create an uplifting and relaxing environment.

Cedarwood

Use to Support These Positive Emotions and Experiences:
Balanced, Calm, Connected, Encouraged, Free, Organized, Present, Relaxed, Soothed

Use to Balance These Negative Emotions and Experiences:
Abused, Bitterness, Debilitated, Over-Stimulated, Panic Disorder, Post-Traumatic Stress Disorder, Self Doubt, Shock, Stress, Stuck, Trauma, Workaholism, Worry

Did you know? Cedarwood has a high level of sesquiterpenes which have been shown to be able to pass the blood brain barrier and have a relaxing effect on the mood.[6]

Experience Cedarwood: Apply 1 drop Cedarwood to the back of the neck, or inhale directly from the bottle to relax the mind.

Cilantro

Use to Support These Positive Emotions and Experiences:
Clear-Minded, Free, Forgiveness, Trusting

Use to Balance These Negative Emotions and Experiences:
Obsessive, Trapped, Worry

Did you know? Aldehydes make up the majority of Cilantro oil. The strong aroma may be off-putting to some users, but others will find the chemistry of this oil to be extremely soothing.

Experience Cilantro: Inhale Cilantro from the bottle and notice how your body responds to the aroma. Try to inhale it beyond the "smell" and remain aware of how your body feels when you inhale it.

Cinnamon

Use to Support These Positive Emotions and Experiences:
Balance, Compromise, Confidence, Free, Healthy Relationships, Happiness, Humility, Independence, Intimacy, Kindness, Relaxed, Self-Acceptance, Sensuality, Strength

Use to Balance These Negative Emotions and Experiences:
Addiction, Alzheimers, Bitterness, Broken Hearted, Codependency, Have to Be Right, Lack of Boundaries, Negative Family Patterns, Parasitic Relationships, Parkinson's Disease, Prideful, Rigid, Self-Righteous, Suicidal, Tourette Syndrome, Unforgiving, Weak-Willed, Worry

Did you know? Just like Cassia oil, Cinnamon has high levels of aldehydes in it, which causes a simultaneously uplifting and calming effect when inhaled.[7]

Experience Cinnamon: Inhale Cinnamon directly from the bottle to enliven the senses and relax the mind.

Clary Sage

Use to Support These Positive Emotions and Experiences:
Clarity, Confidence, Harmony, Inspired, Intuitive, Patience, Positivity, Relaxed, Safety, Self-Approval

Use to Balance These Negative Emotions and Experiences:
Abused, Addicted, Annoyed, Anorexia, Anxiety, Apathy, Bulimia, Debilitated, Depersonalization, Fear, Impatient, Obsessive Compulsive Disorder, Over Eating, Perfectionism, Pessimism, Post-Traumatic Stress Disorder, Stuck, Trauma

Did you know? Clary Sage has a high amount of Esters in it's distilled essential oil, making this oil ideal for relaxation, when anxious or depressed, or before bed if you have trouble sleeping.[8]

Experience Clary Sage: Diffuse Clary Sage to inspire feelings of confidence, positivity, and relaxation.

Clove Bud

Use to Support These Positive Emotions and Experiences:
Healthy Boundaries, Independent, Peacefulness, Protected, Relaxed, Renewed, Responsible

Use to Balance These Negative Emotions and Experiences:
Alzheimers, Codependency, Controlling, Delusions, Lack of Boundaries, Parasitic Relationships, Paranoia, Parkinson's Disease, Phobias, Psychosis, Schizophrenia, Tourette Syndrome

Did you know? Clove oil can be over 80% Phenols, making this oil very sensitive to the skin. This oil is emotionally stimulating due to a strong aroma, try to let the scent waft to you instead of deeply inhaling it, however, inhaling it may also provide neuroprotective effects for the user.[9]

Experience Clove Bud: Inhale lightly from bottle to experience the spicy, energizing aromatic notes of Clove Bud.

Copaiba

Use to Support These Positive Emotions and Experiences:
Balance, Calm, Creativity, Ease, Happiness, Peacefulness, Relaxed, Self-Aware, Self-Compassion

Use to Balance These Negative Emotions and Experiences:
Bipolar Disorder, Conduct Disorder, Delusions, Depression, Embarrassed, Fear, Guilt, Hate, Over Stimulated, Panic Disorder, Paranoia, Parkinson's Disease, Phobias, Psychosis, Post-Traumatic Stress Disorder, Regret, Resignation, Sadness, Schizophrenia, Shame, Stress, Suicidal, Trauma, Tourette Syndrome, Willful-Excessive

Did you know? Copaiba has extremely high levels of sesquiterpenes (can reach over 90%), which are known to penetrate the blood brain barrier to positively impact hormones, mood, and brain. It is also a wonderful oil for reducing inflammation in the body.[10]

Experience Copaiba: Take 1 drop Copaiba under your tongue and hold for 15 seconds and wash down with 4 oz of water to experience the calming effects of this oil on your brain.

Coriander

Use to Support These Positive Emotions and Experiences:
Balance, Calm, Encouraged, Higher Self Alignment, Hopeful, Inspired, Peacefulness

Use to Balance These Negative Emotions and Experiences:
Alzheimers, Annoyed, Bipolar Disorder, Debilitated, Parkinson's Disease, Stuck, Suicidal, Tourette Syndrome

Did you know? Coriander has a high amount of Linalool in it, which makes it ideal for alleviating anxiety, sedating the mind, and soothing inflammation.[11]

Experience Coriander: Inhale Coriander directly from the bottle for 3 deep breaths to experience the soothing aromatic effects of this essential oil.

Cypress

Use to Support These Positive Emotions and Experiences:
Adaptable, Ease, Comfort, Encouragement, Independence, Hope, Healthy Boundaries, Progress, Self Acceptance, Support, Trust

Use to Balance These Negative Emotions and Experiences:
Anxiety, Apathy, Bereavement, Betrayal, Broken Hearted, Codependency, Debilitated, Despair, Discouraged, Fear, Grief, Impatient, Lack of Boundaries, Negative Family Patterns, Parasitic Relationships, Perfectionism, Rejection, Separation Anxiety Disorder, Stuck

Did you know? Cypress has high amounts of Alpha-Pinene in it, making it a great aid for memory support, reducing inflammation, and creating a relaxing environment.

Experience Cypress: Apply 1 drop Cypress over the heart, or on the back of the neck, and inhale it's woodsy, bright aroma to enhance alertness and ease emotional tension.

Douglas Fir

Use to Support These Positive Emotions and Experiences:
Comforted, Confidence, Faith, Focused, Healthy Boundaries, Inclusive, Inspiration, Light-Hearted, Positive, Releasing, Stability, Wisdom

Use to Balance These Negative Emotions and Experiences:
Body Dysmorphia, Codependency, Discourage, Distrusting, Emptiness, Holding Onto The Past, Isolated, Lack of Boundaries, Listless/Lost, Lonely, Materialistic, Negative Family Patterns, Over Serious, Parasitic Relationships, Purposeless, Reclusive, Resentment, Shock, Social Anxiety, Unstable, Upheaval

Did you know? Douglas Fir has high levels of Beta Pinene which helps to alleviate feelings of anxiety and depression and soothes the mind.

Experience Douglas Fir: Apply 1 drop in the palm of your hands and deeply inhale for 5 breaths to experience the fresh, woodsy, holiday memory-inducing scent of Douglas Fir.

Eucalyptus

Use to Support These Positive Emotions and Experiences:
Calm, Clarity, Divinely Guided, Flowing, Focus, Forgiving, Healthy, Organized, Playful, Respectful, Responsible, Self-Assured, Stable, Supported, Tempered

Use to Balance These Negative Emotions and Experiences:
Abused, Addiction, Body Dysmorphia, Bulimia, Confusion, Debilitated, Delusions, Despair, Envy, Has to Be Right, Hoarding, Jealousy, Limiting Beliefs, Listless/Lost, Overeating, Over Serious, Paranoia, Phobias, Prideful, Psychosis, Post-Traumatic Stress Disorder, Purposeless, Rigid, Scarcity, Schizophrenia, Self Doubt, Self Righteous, Stuck, Suicidal, Trauma, Unforgiving, Unstable, Upheaval

Did you know? Eucalyptus is made up primarily of a chemical called 1,8 cineole, which makes it very useful for supporting the respiratory and digestive system and promoting a clear mind.[12]

Experience Eucalyptus: Inhale Eucalyptus from the bottle to refresh your body and mind.

Fennel

Use to Support These Positive Emotions and Experiences:
Harmonizing, Healthy Relationship with Food, Inner Peace, Present, Responsible, Satisfied

Use to Balance These Negative Emotions and Experiences:
Addiction, Bitterness, Bulimia, Overeating, Panic Disorder, Post-Traumatic Stress Disorder, Self Doubt, Trauma, Unhealthy Cravings

Did you know? Fennel may help reduce anxious feelings in users who use it aromatically.[13]

Experience Fennel: Slowly inhale Fennel directly from the bottle, allowing the aroma to come to you to experience it's soothing effects.

Frankincense

Use to Support These Positive Emotions and Experiences:
Aligned, Calm, Focus, Intuitive, Loved, Manifesting, Peace, Resilient, Unashamed, Whole

Use to Balance These Negative Emotions and Experiences:
Abused, ADHD, Anger, Anzlheimers, Annoyed, Anxiety, Autism, Bereavement, Betrayal, Bipolar Disorder, Broken Hearted, Bulimia, Codependency, Confusion, Controlling, Critical, Debilitated, Delusions, Depression, Despair, Envy, Emptiness, Fear, Grief, Hate, Impatient, Isolated, Limiting Beliefs, Lost,Obsessive Compulsive Disorder, Over Stimulated, Panic Disorder, Parkinson's Disease, Perfectionism, Phobias, Prideful, Psychosis, Rage, Resentment, Rigid, Sadness, Scarcity, Scattered, Schizophrenia, Self Righteous, Shock, Social Anxiety, Stress, Suicidal, Trauma, Tourette Syndrome, Unstable, Willful--Excessive, Workaholism, Worry

Did you know? Frankincense amplifies the effects of other oils mixed with it and it is a wonderful support for reducing feelings of anxiety, depression, and fatigue.[14]

Experience Frankincense: Inhale directly from bottle, or place 1 drop under tongue.

Geranium

Use to Support These Positive Emotions and Experiences:
Body Positivity, Comfort, Confidence, Focus, Happiness, Heart Healing, Peace, Relaxed, Serenity, Support

Use to Balance These Negative Emotions and Experiences:
Addiction, ADD/ADHD, Anger, Annoyed, Bereavement, Betrayal, Broken Hearted, Bulimia, Despair, Discouraged, Envy, Emptiness, Fear, Grief, Hate, Isolated, Jealousy, Lonely, Overeating, Panic Disorder, Paranoia, Psychosis, Rage, Reclusive, Rejection, Scattered, Self Doubt, Shock, Unforgiving, Worry

Did you know? Geranium has Linalool in it, which makes it an excellent stress reliever, anxiety reducer, sedative, and anti-inflammatory essential oil.[15]

Experience Geranium: Apply 1 drop of Geranium over the heart and deeply inhale to feel the nurturing effects of this special oil.

Ginger

Use to Support These Positive Emotions and Experiences:
Body Positivity, Ease, Enthusiasm, Focus, Passion, Vitality

Use to Balance These Negative Emotions and Experiences:
Apathy, Bulimia, Debilitated, Discouraged, Overeating, Shock, Stuck, Weak-Willed

Did you know? Ginger oil has high levels of Zingiberene in it, which supports healthy blood pressure levels and is an antioxidant to the body.

Experience Ginger: Place 1 drop of Ginger oil with a squeeze of lemon juice in 12oz of cold water to experience the vivacious energy of this essential oil.

Grapefruit

Use to Support These Positive Emotions and Experiences:
Body Positivity, Excitement, Elevation, Expansion, Forgiveness, Happiness, Humility, Wholeness

Use to Balance These Negative Emotions and Experiences:
ADD/ADHD, Anger, Alzheimers, Annoyed, Anxiety, Betrayal, Bipolar Disorder, Codependency, Conduct Disorder, Controlling, Critical, Delusions, Distrusting, Envy, Emptiness, Focus, Frustrated, Have to Be Right, Jealousy, Lack of Boundaries, Limiting Beliefs, Obsessive Compulsive, Over Serious, Over Stimulated, Parasitic Relationships, Panic Disorder, Paranoia, Parkinson's Disease, Perfectionism, Pessimism, Phobias, Prideful, Psychosis, Rage, Rejection, Rigid, Sadness, Scattered, Schizophrenia, Self-Righteous, Separation Anxiety, Social Anxiety, Stress, Tourette Syndrome, Unstable, Upheaval, Weak Willed, Willful--Excessive, Workaholism, Worry

Did you know? Grapefruit's high level of d-Limonene makes this oil an ideal resource for alleviating anxiety, stress, inflammation, and helps to soothe digestion.[16]

Experience Grapefruit: Inhale Grapefruit directly from the bottle to experience the juicy, bright, punch of fruity deliciousness that alleviates anxiety, depression, and delights the senses.

Green Mandarin

Use to Support These Positive Emotions and Experiences:
Ease, Fluidity, Hopeful, Positive, Relaxed

Use to Balance These Negative Emotions and Experiences:
Have to Be Right, Prideful, Rigid, Self Righteous, Unforgiving

Did you know? Green Mandarin is over 75% Limonene, which packs a major boost of stress-relieving aromatic benefits and has lightly soothing notes that will tame anxious feelings.

Experience Green Mandarin: Inhale Green Mandarin directly from the bottle for an aromatherapy experience that leaves you feeling refreshed and relaxed.

Helichrysum

Use to Support These Positive Emotions and Experiences:
At Ease, Grounding, Hopeful, Momentum, Soothing, Rapid Healing, Regenerating, Relaxed

Use to Balance These Negative Emotions and Experiences:
Abused, Delusions, Gender Dysphoria, Paranoia, Phobias, Psychosis, Post Traumatic Stress Disorder, Resentment, Schizophrenia, Trauma

Did you know? Helichrysum is referred to as "stitches in a bottle" because of it's highly regenerative nature on the skin. Apply it to any cut or wound for rapid healing. Use it aromatically for reducing mental fatigue and burnout.[17]

Experience Helichrysum: Apply 1 drop of Helichrysum directly over heart and deeply inhale to relax the mind and body while comforting and soothing an upset emotional state.

Jasmine

Use to Support These Positive Emotions and Experiences:
Appreciative, Body Positive, Clarity, Confident, Emotional Strength, Encouraged, Focused, Positivity, Relaxed, Sensual, Secure, Supported

Use to Balance These Negative Emotions and Experiences:
Abused, Anorexia, Body Dysmorphia, Bulimia, Disconnected, Discouraged, Isolated, Listless/Lost, Lonely, Materialistic, Overeating, Panic Disorder, Post Traumatic Stress Disorder, Purposeless, Reclusive, Self Doubt, Shock, Suicidal, Trauma

Did you know? Jasmine is a soft, feminine essential oil that enhances confidence and inner strength.[18] It is ideal for boosting confidence around intimacy. It's also great for relieving depression and uplifting one's mood.[19]

Experience Jasmine: Apply Jasmine over heart and deeply inhale to receive the support that this essential oil provides.

Juniper Berry

Use to Support These Positive Emotions and Experiences:
Abundance, Attention, Energized, Individuation, Peaceful, Safety, Supported

Use to Balance These Negative Emotions and Experiences:
Abused, Addiction, Annoyed, Apathy, Debilitated, Discouraged, Envy, Fear, Jealousy, Limiting Beliefs, Night Terrors, Post Traumatic Stress Disorder, Self Doubt, Stuck, Trauma, Worry

Did you know? Juniper Berry has high amounts of Monoterpenes, like Alpha-Pinene, which helps support memory and relaxation.

Experience Juniper Berry: Diffuse Juniper Berry to create a peaceful, calm environment to support a stable emotional state.

Lavender

Use to Support These Positive Emotions and Experiences:
Acceptance, Communication, Decrease Heart-Rate, Enhance Focus, Feelings of Ease, Lower Cortisol, Peacefulness, Relaxation, Reduce Experience of Physical Pain

Use to Balance These Negative Emotions and Experiences:
Abuse, Anger, Anxiety, Betrayal, Codependency, Confusion, Delusions, Depression, Fear, Frustration, Insomnia, Isolation, Lack of Trust, Limiting Beliefs, Need to Control, Obsessive Pessimism, Stress, Thoughts, Trauma

Did you know? Lavender's high levels of linalool help facilitate a relaxing experience for users and its high levels of linalyl acetate helps with lowering inflammation and reducing pain.[20]

Experience Lavender: Apply 1-2 drops Lavender to back of neck or temples to relieve stress and headaches caused by stress.

Lemon

Use to Support These Positive Emotions and Experiences:
Ease, Energy, Focus, Happiness, Joyful, Mental Clarity,
Optimism

Use to Balance These Negative Emotions and Experiences:

ADD/ADHD, Anger, Alzheimers, Annoyed, Anxiety, Apathy,
Autism/Aspergers, Bereavement, Betrayal, Bipolar, Bitterness,
Broken Hearted, Bulimia, Conduct Disorder, Confusion,
Controlling, Critical, Delusions, Depression, Despair, Difficulty
with Transitions, Distrusting, Envy, Emptiness, Fear, Frustrated,
Grief, Have to Be Right, Hate, Hoarding, Impatient, Jealousy,
Limiting Belief, Listless/Lost, Materialistic, Negative Family
Patterns, Obsessive Compulsive, Overeating, Over Serious,
Over Stimulated, Panic Disorder, Paranoia, Parkinson's
Disease, Pessimism, Phobias, Prideful, Psychosis, Post
Traumatic Stress Disorder, Purposeless, Rage, Resignation,
Rigid, Sadness, Scarcity, Scattered, Schizophrenia, Self Doubt,
Lemon, Separation Anxiety Disorder, Shock, Social Anxiety,
Stress, Trauma, Tourette Syndrome, Unforgiving, Unstable,
Upheaval, Willful--Excessive, Workaholism

Did you know? Lemon has extremely high amounts of
D-Limonene in it, which makes it a wonderful stress reliever,
antidepressant, and anxiety reducer.[21]

Experience Lemon: Apply 1 drop to palms of hands and
deeply inhale to uplift mood and mental clarity.

Lemongrass

Use to Support These Positive Emotions and Experiences:
Clarity, Healthy Boundaries, Independence, Self Direction

Use to Balance These Negative Emotions and Experiences:
Codependency, Debilitated, Discouraged, Lack of Boundaries,
Parasitic Relationships, Stuck, Weak-Willed

Did you know? Lemongrass is comprised of Aldehydes which
both soothes and uplifts users.[22]

Experience Lemongrass: Inhale Lemongrass directly from
bottle for clarity and energy.

Lime

Use to Support These Positive Emotions and Experiences:
Balance, Energy, Flexibility, Healthy Boundaries, Joy, Uplifted, Zestful

Use to Balance These Negative Emotions and Experiences:
Abused, Addiction, Anorexia, Anxiety, Bipolar, Codependency, Depression, Discouraged, Holding Onto The Past, Listless/Lost, Over Serious, Parasitic Relationship, Pessimistic, Post Traumatic Stress Disorder, Purposeless, Separation Anxiety Disorder, Social Anxiety, Trauma

Did you know? Lime, just like Lemon, has extremely high amounts of D-Limonene in it, which make it a wonderful stress reliever and anxiety reducer.

Experience Lime: Diffuse Lime oil to bring a bright, vivacious, uplifting energy to your mood and environment.

Litsea

Use to Support These Positive Emotions and Experiences:
Alignment, Confidence, Inner Wisdom, Momentum

Use to Balance These Negative Emotions and Experiences:
Gender Dysphoria, Rejected, Self Doubt, Stuck

Did you know? Litsea and Lemongrass have very similar aromatic profiles. This is due to the fact that both of them are comprised of mostly Aldehydes and they are both anti-inflammatories.[23]

Experience Litsea: Diffuse Litsea for inspiration and alignment with one's true purpose.

Magnolia

Use to Support These Positive Emotions and Experiences:
Aligned, Balanced, Connected, Enlivened, Hopeful, Peaceful, Rested, Surrendered

Use to Balance These Negative Emotions and Experiences:

Abused, Anorexia, Autism/Aspergers, Body Dysmorphia, Depersonalization, Disconnected, Gender Dysphoria, Hoarding, Insomnia, Listless/Lost, Materialistic, Night Terrors, Post Traumatic Stress Disorder, Suicidal, Trauma, Workaholism, Worry

Did you know? Magnolia comes from a tree known as the "white jade orchid tree" and has a beautiful, well-rounded scent that is slightly sweet with a hint of tartness. It has high levels of Eucalyptol, which passes the blood brain barrier and carries messages of relaxation to the brain and provides neuroprotection.

Experience Magnolia: Apply Magnolia to wrists and neck to feel inspired, aligned, and at peace.

Manuka

Use to Support These Positive Emotions and Experiences:
Aligned, Comforted, Connected, Grounded, Strength

Use to Balance These Negative Emotions and Experiences:
Disconnected, Gender Dysphoria, Grief, Weak-Willed

Did you know? Manuka oil has a high level of Sesquiterpenes in it which have major calming properties and help support neurological health.

Experience Manuka: Apply Manuka oil to hands and inhale for a grounding, comforting effect.

Marjoram

Use to Support These Positive Emotions and Experiences:
Anticipation, Healthy Boundaries, Hopeful, Inspired, Peace, Relaxed, Self-Assuredness, Surrender

Use to Balance These Negative Emotions and Experiences:
Bereavement, Betrayal, Broken Hearted, Codependency, Controlling, Despair, Fear, Grief, Lack of Boundaries, Obsessive Compulsive Behavior, Parasitic Relationships, Panic Disorder, Rejection, Worry

Did you know? Marjoram is mostly Monoterpenes, which have been proven to fight certain cancers and be an incredible anti-inflammatory. Marjoram has been shown in certain studies to reduce pain, anxiety, stress, and depression.[24]

Experience Marjoram: Diffuse Marjoram to inspire an atmosphere of hope and confidence.

Melissa

Use to Support These Positive Emotions and Experiences:
Body Positivity, Hope, Inspired, Peace, Positivity, Release, Sanity, Safety, Self-Acceptance

Use to Balance These Negative Emotions and Experiences:
Abused, Bereavement, Betrayal, Bipolar Disorder, Body Dysmorphia, Broken Hearted, Conduct Disorder, Confusion, Delusions, Depression, Despair, Fear, Grief, Panic Disorder, Paranoia, Phobias, Psychosis, Post Traumatic Stress Disorder, Rejection, Schizophrenia, Suicidal, Trauma, Worry

Did you know? Melissa is mostly Aldehydes, which simultaneously causes an uplifting and calming effect when the essential oil is inhaled.[25]

Experience Melissa: Inhale Melissa directly from bottle to get a burst of energy and positivity from its spicy, warm aroma.

Myrrh

Use to Support These Positive Emotions and Experiences:
Independence, Healthy Relationships, Peace, Rooted, Self Confidence

Use to Balance These Negative Emotions and Experiences:
Codependency, Controlling, Isolated, Lack of Boundaries, Negative Family Patterns, Obsessive Compulsive Disorder, Parasitic Relationships, Reclusive, Resentment

Did you know? Myrrh has a high level of sesquiterpenes, which have been shown to be able to pass the blood brain barrier and have a relaxing effect on the mood.

Experience Myrrh: Diffuse Myrrh to create a relaxing and nourishing effect on the brain and your mood.

Neroli

Use to Support These Positive Emotions and Experiences:
Calm, Happiness, Intimacy, Patience, Peace, Relaxed, Resilient, Supported

Use to Balance These Negative Emotions and Experiences:
Abused, Anxiety, Autism/Aspergers, Bereavement, Betrayal, Bitterness, Broken Hearted, Despair, Grief, Isolated, Lonely, Panic, Post Traumatic Stress Disorder, Reclusive, Rejection, Trauma, Worry

Did you know? Neroli has a high level of Monoterpenes in it and is a fabulous oil for supporting an upbeat and resilient mood, lowering blood pressure, and increasing sexual desire.[26]

Experience Neroli: Apply Neroli on the back of the neck and over the heart and deeply inhale to experience it's uplifting and emotionally soothing properties.

Oregano

Use to Support These Positive Emotions and Experiences:
Balance, Energy, Happiness, Positivity

Use to Balance These Negative Emotions and Experiences:
Bipolar, Depresion, Negativity, Pessimism

Did you know? Oregano, when taken internally, has been scientifically shown to improve mood? It's high levels of Carvacrol make this happen and also boost the immune system.[27]

Experience Oregano: Place 1 drop of Oregano in a vegetable capsule and take twice a day with food to help support your mood and immune system.

Patchouli

Use to Support These Positive Emotions and Experiences:
Confident, Grounding, Hopeful, Inner Strength, Uplifting

Use to Balance These Negative Emotions and Experiences:
Abused, Alzheimers, Debilitated, Despair, Post Traumatic Stress Disorder, Self Doubt, Stuck, Trauma, Tourette Syndrome

Did you know? Patchouli has a high level of Sesquiterpenes which have been shown to be able to pass the blood brain barrier and have a relaxing yet uplifting effect on the mood.[28]

Experience Patchouli: Inhale Patchouli directly from the bottle to experience its grounding, stabilizing, uplifting effects.

Peppermint

Use to Support These Positive Emotions and Experiences:
Cognitive Performance, Energized, Happiness, Levity, Open Minded, Relief, Refreshed

Use to Balance These Negative Emotions and Experiences:
ADD/ADHD, Aloof, Anger, Annoyed, Anorexia, Apathy, Betrayal, Bipolar, Conduct Disorder, Confusion, Debilitated, Delusions, Depersonalization, Depression, Despair, Difficulty with Transitions, Disconnected, Embarrassed, Focus, Frustrated, Guilt, Hoarding, Isolated, Paranoia, Phobias, Psychosis, Rage, Reclusive, Regret, Resignation, Rejection, Sadness, Scarcity, Scattered, Schizophrenia, Self Doubt, Shame, Suicidal, Worry

Did you know? Peppermint has been shown to reduce daytime sleepiness, enhance memory and cognitive performance, and it's significant levels of Menthone have been shown to be an antidepressant.

Experience Peppermint: Place 1 drop of Peppermint oil in 12oz of water and drink to experience the refreshing, energizing, and brain-boosting effects of this special oil!

Petitgrain

Use to Support These Positive Emotions and Experiences:
Confidence, Identity, Positivity, Productivity, Security

Use to Balance These Negative Emotions and Experiences:
Gender Dysphoria, Insomnia, Night Terrors, Pessimism

Did you know? Petitgrain's uplifting effect on the mood have been linked to increased workplace productivity.[30] Use this oil when you want to feel at ease and make a positive impact on those around you!

Experience Petitgrain: Diffuse Petitgrain or inhale directly from the bottle to experience it's wonderful effects on the central nervous system.

Roman Chamomile

Use to Support These Positive Emotions and Experiences:
Confidence, Divinity, Fulfilled, Joy, Peace, Purpose, Serenity

Use to Balance These Negative Emotions and Experiences:
Abused, Anger, Alzheimers, Annoyed, Anxiety, Betrayal, Codependency, Controlling, Delusions, Envy, Gender Dysphoria, Hate, Jealousy, Lack of Boundaries, Limiting Beliefs, Obsessive Compulsive Disorder, Over Stimulated, Parasitic Relationships, Panic Disorder, Paranoia, Parkinson's Disease, Phobias, Psychosis, Post Traumatic Stress Disorder, Rage, Rejection, Resentment, Schizophrenia, Separation Anxiety Disorder, Shock, Social Anxiety, Stress, Trauma, Tourette Syndrome, Workaholism, Worry

Did you know? Studies show that Roman Chamomile reduces anxiety, improves sleep, and is an effective antidepressant.

Experience Roman Chamomile: Place 1 drop of Roman Chamomile in the palms of your hands and deeply inhale aroma.

Rose

Use to Support These Positive Emotions and Experiences:
Amorous, Comforted, Decreased Heart Rate, Healed, Intimacy, Relaxed, Supported

Use to Balance These Negative Emotions and Experiences:
Abused, Addiction, Anxiety, Bereavement, Betrayal, Bipolar, Broken Hearted, Delusions, Despair, Emptiness, Fear, Grief, Hoarding, Listless/lost, Materialistic, Panic Disorder, Paranoia, Pessimism, Phobias, Psychosis, Purposeless, Resentment, Schizophrenia, Self Doubt, Separation Anxiety, Shock, Social Anxiety, Suicidal, Worry

Did you know? Rose has been shown to decrease blood pressure, heart rate, and be a reliable tool for easing anxiety and depression.[32] It also enhances sexual function and intimacy.[33]

Experience Rose: Apply Rose over the heart and deeply inhale its aroma for 5 breaths.

Rosemary

Use to Support These Positive Emotions and Experiences:
Clarity, Energy, Flexible, Focus, Optimism, Rejuvenated, Vitality

Use to Balance These Negative Emotions and Experiences:
Abused, Addiction, ADD/ADHD, Aloof, Anger, Annoyed, Anorexia, Apathy, Betrayal, Bipolar, Bitterness, Bulimia, Confusion, Critical, Debilitated, Delusions, Depersonalization, Depression, Despair, Difficulty With Transition, Disconnected, Discouraged, Focus, Hoarding, Listless/Lost, Overeating, Panic Disorder, Paranoia, Phobias, Psychosis, Post Traumatic Stress Disorder, Purposeless, Rage, Resignation, Rejection, Sadness, Scattered, Schizophrenia, Self Doubt, Stuck, Suicidal, Trauma, Weak Willed

Did you know? Rosemary has been shown to enhance memory, reduce cortisol, and reduce depression and stress.[34]

Experience Rosemary: Inhale Rosemary directly from the bottle to experience its vivacious, mentally clarifying aroma.

Sandalwood

Use to Support These Positive Emotions and Experiences:
Comforting, Connection, Relaxing, Rest, Sedating, Spiritual Connection

Use to Balance These Negative Emotions and Experiences:
Alzheimers, Autism/Aspergers, Controlling, Discouraged, Insomnia, Isolated, Limiting Beliefs, Negative Family Patterns, Night Terrors, Obsessive Compulsive Behavior, Overstimulated, Parkinson's Disease, Reclusive, Scarcity, Self Doubt, Stress, Tourette Syndrom, Workaholism

Did you know? Sandalwood is great for sedating the body and reducing fatigue.

Experience Sandalwood: Apply Sandalwood to the back of the neck and deeply inhale the residual aroma that remains on the hands for 5 deep breaths.

Siberian Fir

Use to Support These Positive Emotions and Experiences:
Alert, Confidence, Grounded, Healthy Boundaries, Independent, Resilient, Trusting

Use to Balance These Negative Emotions and Experiences:
Bitterness, Body Dysmorphia, Codependency, Distrusting, Emptiness, Hoarding, Lack of Boundaries, Negative Family Patterns, Parasitic Relationships, Resentment, Unstable, Upheaval

Did you know? Siberian Fir has a high amount of Monoterpenes Camphene, Alpha-Pinene, and Beta-Pinene which all help to support memory and promote relaxation.

Experience Siberian Fir: Diffuse SIberian Fir while working or focusing on a task to enhance your mental performance and give you energy to complete the task.

Spearmint

Use to Support These Positive Emotions and Experiences:
Clarity, Coherent, Positivity, Self-Assured, Uplifted

Use to Balance These Negative Emotions and Experiences:
Abused, Addiction, Bipolar, Body Dysmorphia, Bulimia, Delusions, Hate, Overeating, Panic Disorder, Paranoia, Phobias, Psychosis, Post Traumatic Stress Disorder, Resentment, Schizophrenia, Trauma, Unstable, Worry

Did you know? Spearmint has been shown by researchers to reduce manic-like symptoms, reduce anxiety, stress, and help to sedate the user.[44]

Experience Spearmint: Diffuse Spearmint to create a peaceful environment with uplifting vibes.

Spikenard

Use to Support These Positive Emotions and Experiences:
Peaceful, Proper Pacing of Life, Rested, Sound Mind

Use to Balance These Negative Emotions and Experiences:
Abused, Bipolar, Delusions, Insomnia, Night Terrors, Over Stimulated, Paranoia, Phobias, Psychosis, Post-Traumatic Stress Disorder, Schizophrenia, Stress, Trauma, Workaholism

Did you know? Studies have shown Spikenard to be very sedating and help to prolong periods of restful sleep.[36]

Experience Spikenard: Diffuse 1-2 drops Spikenard while falling asleep to help promote a restful sleeping experience.

Tangerine

Use to Support These Positive Emotions and Experiences:
Cheerful, Creative, Optimistic, Peaceful, Uplifted

Use to Balance These Negative Emotions and Experiences:
Anxiety, Bipolar, Overstimulated, Panic Disorder, Perfectionism, Scarcity, Separation Anxiety Disorder, Social Anxiety, Stress, Suicidal, Workaholism

Did you know? Tangerine has been reported to help regulate emotions such as stress, overly-anxious, depression, or fretfulness.

Experience Tangerine: Diffuse Tangerine to experience a burst of citrus aroma that uplifts the spirit and reinvigorates the mind.

Tea Tree

Use to Support These Positive Emotions and Experiences:
Empowered, Healthy Boundaries, Security

Use to Balance These Negative Emotions and Experiences:
Codependency, Fear, Lack of Boundaries, Parasitic Relationships

Did you know? Tea Tree chemistry profile is comprised of over half Monoterpenes, making this essential oil potentially useful for relaxation.

Experience Tea Tree: Apply 1 drop Tea Tree to wrists to provide energetic boundaries and protection from others' energy.

Turmeric

Use to Support These Positive Emotions and Experiences:
Balance, Energy, Gumption, Momentum

Use to Balance These Negative Emotions and Experiences:
Abused, Betrayal, Stuck, Trauma

Did you know? Turmeric is a powerful antioxidant and anti-inflammatory agent and taking this oil internally helps to support mood from the inside-out.

Experience Turmeric: Take 1 drop of Turmeric in a vegetable capsule with food twice daily to help support your mood and immune system.

Thyme

Use to Support These Positive Emotions and Experiences:
Fortitude, Identity, Momentum, Present, Self Awareness, Visibility

Use to Balance These Negative Emotions and Experiences:
Aloof, Anorexia, Debilitated, Depersonalization, Disconnected, Discouraged, Hoarding, Isolated, Lonely, Reclusive, Self Doubt, Stuck

Did you know? Taking Thyme internally can boost feelings of well-being, confidence, and optimism due to its high levels of Carvacrol.[38]

Experience Thyme: Take 1 drop of Thyme in a vegetable capsule with food twice daily to experience the uplifting effects of this oil.

Vetiver

Use to Support These Positive Emotions and Experiences:
Assuredness, Peaceful, Rested, Surrender, Trusting

Use to Balance These Negative Emotions and Experiences:
Bipolar, Conduct Disorder, Controlling, Delusions, Distrusting, Fear, Frustrated, Have to Be Right, Hoarding, Insomnia, Night Terrors, Obsessive Compulsive Behavior, Over Stimulated, Panic Disorder, Paranoia, Phobias, Prideful, Psychosis, Resentment, Rigid, Schizophrenia, Self Righteous, Shock, Social Anxiety, Stress, Unforgiving, Willful--Excessive, Workaholism, Worry

Did you know? Vetiver is helpful for reducing anxiety and increasing restful sleep.[39] Interestingly, at low doses it has also been shown to enhance focus.[40]

Experience Vetiver: Diffuse Vetiver before bed to help you relax and drift off to a restful sleep. Inhale 1-2 breaths from the bottle of Vetiver to relax an overactive mind and allow yourself to focus.

Wild Orange

Use to Support These Positive Emotions and Experiences:
Abundance, Ease, Energy, Focus, Happiness, Joyful, Mental Clarity, Optimism, Playfulness

Use to Balance These Negative Emotions and Experiences:
ADD/ADHD, Anger, Alzheimers, Annoyed, Anxiety, Apathy, Autism/Aspergers, Bereavement, Betrayal, Bipolar, Bitterness, Broken Hearted, Bulimia, Conduct Disorder, Confusion, Controlling, Critical, Delusions, Depression, Despair, Difficulty with Transitions, Distrusting, Envy, Emptiness, Fear, Frustrated, Grief, Have to Be Right, Hate, Hoarding, Impatient, Limiting Belief, Listless/Lost, Materialistic, Negative Family Patterns, Obsessive Compulsive, Overeating, Over Serious, Over Stimulated, Panic Disorder, Paranoia, Parkinson's Disease, Pessimism, Phobias, Prideful, Psychosis, Post Traumatic Stress Disorder, Purposeless, Rage, Resignation, Rigid, Scarcity, Scattered, Schizophrenia, Self Doubt, Lemon, Shock, Social Anxiety, Stress, Trauma, Tourette Syndrome, Unforgiving, Unstable, Upheaval, Willful--Excessive, Workaholism

Did you know? Wild Orange may reduce anxiety, lower cortisol, and help lower stress during labor.[41]

Experience Wild Orange: Place 1 drop of Wild Orange in your hands for a happier mood.

Wintergreen

Use to Support These Positive Emotions and Experiences:
Healthy Boundaries, Overcoming, Resilience, Self Acceptance

Use to Balance These Negative Emotions and Experiences:
Betrayal, Codependency, Hoarding, Parasitic Relationships, Rejection

Did you know? Due to being commonly found in gum and mints, the aroma of Wintergreen might remind you of something familiar. This is because of the strong memory in our olfactory system that ties memories to smells.

Experience Wintergreen: Inhale Wintergreen directly from the bottle for a quick mood boost.

Yarrow | Pom

Use to Support These Positive Emotions and Experiences:
Healthy Boundaries, Organized, Security, Safety

Use to Balance These Negative Emotions and Experiences:
Codependency, Debilitated, Hoarding, Scattered

Did you know? According to research, Yarrow has a soothing anti-anxiety effect on users.[42]

Experience Yarrow | Pom: Apply Yarrow | Pom on neck and chest, massaging into skin for a soothing, relaxing effect.

Ylang Ylang

Use to Support These Positive Emotions and Experiences:
Decreased Blood Pressure, Forgiving, Joyful, Loved, Nourished, Peaceful, Supported

Use to Balance These Negative Emotions and Experiences:
Abused, Addiction, Aloof, Anorexia, Bipolar, Bulimia, Delusions, Depersonalization, Disconnected, Envy, Embarrassed, Emptiness, Fear, Guilt, Have to Be Right, Hate, Insomnia, Isolated, Jealousy, Lonely, Night Terrors, Overeating, Over Stimulated, Panic Disorder, Paranoia, Perfectionism, Phobias, Prideful, Psychosis, Post Traumatic Stress Disorder, Reclusive, Regret, Rigid, Schizophrenia, Self Doubt, Self Righteous, Shame, Stress, Suicidal, Trauma, Unforgiving, Workaholism

Did you know? According to research, Ylang Ylang reduces stress, depression, and lowers blood pressure.[43]

Experience Ylang Ylang: Apply 1 drop of Ylang Ylang over your heart to nourish yourself and feel the relaxing, soothing aroma of this essential oil as it supports you.

Anti-Aging Blend

Use to Support These Positive Emotions and Experiences:
Abundance, Belief in Possibilities, Body Positivity, Connected to Self, Grounded, Security, Spiritual Connection

Use to Balance These Negative Emotions and Experiences:
Body Dysmorphia, Broken Hearted, Limiting Beliefs, Materialistic, Scarcity

Ingredients: Frankincense Resin, Hawaiian Sandalwood, Lavender Flower, Myrrh Gum Resin, Helichrysum Flower, Rose Flower essential oils

Experience Anti-Aging Blend: Apply Anti-Aging Blend over your heart to support feeling spiritually connected, abundant, and grounded.

Blend for Women

Use to Support These Positive Emotions and Experiences:
Balancing, Body Positivity, Intimacy, Self Acceptance, Self Love

Use to Balance These Negative Emotions and Experiences:
Gender Dysphoria, Self Doubt

Ingredients: Fractionated Coconut Oil, Patchouli Leaf, Bergamot Peel, Hawaiian Sandalwood Wood, Rose Flower, Vanilla Bean Absolute, Jasmine Flower, Cinnamon Bark, Vetiver Root, Labdanum Leaf/Stem, Cocoa Seed, Ylang Ylang Flower

Did You Know? This blend interacts with the pH on your skin and will smell differently on each person who wears it as perfume.

Experience Blend for Women: Apply 1 drop of Blend for Women on wrists to enhance your mood and balance masculine and feminine energy. Use in place of perfume.

Captivating Blend

Use to Support These Positive Emotions and Experiences:
Grounding, Self Confidence, Uplifting

Use to Balance These Negative Emotions and Experiences:
Aloof, Annoyed, Bitterness, Discouraged, Distrusting, Emptiness, Frustrated, Limiting Beliefs, Purposeless

Ingredients: Fractionated Coconut Oil, Lime Peel, Osmanthus Flower, Bergamot, and Frankincense essential oils

Did You Know? Each of these oils in this blend are highly elevating to the mood and this is a great go-to oil for many emotional needs to support a positive mood state.

Experience Inspiring Blend: Apply Inspiring Blend to wrists or palms and deeply inhale for an uplifting, comforting aroma that instills self confidence.

Cellular Complex Blend

Use to Support These Positive Emotions and Experiences:
Brain Health, Inner Peace, Inner Stamina, Openness

Use to Balance These Negative Emotions and Experiences:
Alzheimers, Debilitated, Parkinson's Disease, Tourette Syndrome

Ingredients: Frankincense Resin, Wild Orange Peel, Litsea Fruit, Thyme Leaf, Clove Bud, Summer Savory Plant, Niaouli Leaf, and Lemongrass Leaf essential oils

Did You Know? This oil has powerful effects on cells and aids in producing healthy cellular apoptosis.

Experience Cellular Complex: Take 1-2 Cellular Complex Softgels twice daily internally to experience the whole-body support of this essential oil. Inhale directly from bottle for a spicy, warm burst of aroma.

Centering Blend

Use to Support These Positive Emotions and Experiences: Grounded, Healing, Open to New Possibilities, Self Acceptance, Self Awareness

Use to Balance These Negative Emotions and Experiences: Bereavement, Betrayal, Broken Hearted, Despair, Grief, Rejection

Ingredients: Bergamot, Coriander, Marjoram, Peppermint, Jasmine absolute, and Rose essential oils in a base of Fractionated Coconut Oil

Did You Know? This essential oil is great for being used as part of a meditation, a spiritual practice, or during yoga.

Experience Centering Blend: Apply Centering Blend to palms of hands and deeply inhale for 5 breaths to bring an anxious mind or sad heart back to a place of stillness and wholeness.

Cleansing Blend

Use to Support These Positive Emotions and Experiences: Acceptance, Delight, Peace, Spaciousness, Surrender

Use to Balance These Negative Emotions and Experiences: Controlling, Hate, Hoarding, Rage

Ingredients: Lemon Peel, Siberian Fir Needle, Citronella Grass, Lime Peel, Melaleuca (Tea Tree) Leaf, Cilantro Herb essential oils.

Did You Know? Due to the high amount of lemon in this blend, this essential oil is great for getting rid of stubborn aromas in the air of your home and replacing it with a clean, fresh scent.

Experience Cleansing Blend: Diffuse the Cleaning Blend in your home, office, bedroom, or bathroom to cleanse the space and clear the energy.

Comforting Blend

Use to Support These Positive Emotions and Experiences:
Acceptance, Comfort, Communal Support, Forgiveness, Identity, Letting Go, Love, Soothing, Support

Use to Balance These Negative Emotions and Experiences:
Abused, Addiction, Anger, Bipolar, Bitterness, Body Dysmorphia, Broken Hearted, Codependency, Debilitated, Despair, Discouraged, Embarrassed, Emptiness, Gender Dysphoria, Grief, Guilt, Hate, Hoarding, Lonely Negative, Parasitic Relationships, Pessimism, Post Traumatic Stress, Regret, Resentment, Sadness, Shame, Shock, Suicidal, Trauma, Unforgiving, Upheaval

Ingredients: Frankincense Resin, Patchouli Leaf, Ylang Ylang Flower, Labdanum Stem/Twig, Amyris Bark, Sandalwood Wood, Rose Flower, Osmanthus Flower

Did You Know? The Ylang Ylang, Patchouli, and Frankincense in this blend create stress-relieving, antidepressant qualities.[45]

Experience Comforting Blend: Apply Comforting Blend on your chest to nurture and nourish your emotional heart when it's feeling sad, weighed down, and burdened.

Detoxification Blend

Use to Support These Positive Emotions and Experiences:
Cleansing, Detox, Enthusiasm, Freedom, Optimism, Purification, Momentum

Use to Balance These Negative Emotions and Experiences:
Addiction, Apathy, Limiting Beliefs, Stuck

Ingredients: Tangerine Peel, Rosemary Leaf, Geranium Flower/Leaf, Juniper Berry, Cilantro Herb essential oils

Did You Know? Some people experience emotional shifts and relief when going through a detoxification process. This blend helps to facilitate both a physical detox and emotional detox.

Experience Detoxification Blend: Apply 2 drops of Detoxification Blend to the bottom of your feet to begin shifting energetic patterns in your body and in your surrounding environment.

Digestive Blend

Use to Support These Positive Emotions and Experiences:
Acceptance, Acknowledging, Energy, Fortitude, Peace,
Processing Information

Use to Balance These Negative Emotions and Experiences:
Bulimia, Fear, Overeating, Shock, Tension, Weak-Willed

Ingredients: Anise Seed, Peppermint Plant, Ginger Rhizome/
Root, Caraway Seed, Coriander Seed, Tarragon Plant, and
Fennel Seed essential oils

Did You Know? Our stomach can hold a lot of tension when
we are emotionally stressed, so having an essential oil that
relieves tension and soothes digestion can be a huge help for
emotional processing.

Experience Digestive Blend: Apply a few drops of Digestive
Blend around navel and inhale aroma leftover on hands to
promote a healthy emotional digestive experience.

Encouraging Blend

Use to Support These Positive Emotions and Experiences:
Anticipation, Comforted, Connected, Excitement, Optimistic,
Stable, Supported, Upbeat

Use to Balance These Negative Emotions and Experiences:
Aloof, Anorexia, Apathy, Bipolar, Depersonalization,
Depression, Disconnected, Envy, Isolated, Jealousy, Limiting
Beliefs, Lonely, Reclusive, Resignation, Stuck

Ingredients: Fractionated Coconut Oil, Peppermint Plant,
Clementine Peel, Coriander Seed, Basil Herb, Yuzu Peel,
Melissa Leaf, Rosemary Leaf, Vanilla Bean Absolute

Did You Know? The Melissa Oil in this blend helps to make
this a very therapeutic oil for alleviating agitation, depression,
and lowering heart rate.[46]

Experience Encouraging Blend: Diffuse Encouraging Blend
to promote and optimistic mood when you need to get things
done, or overcome a difficult challenge that requires taking
action.

Enlightening Blend

Use to Support These Positive Emotions and Experiences:
Awareness, Calm, Relaxed, Self-Confidence, Stability

Use to Balance These Negative Emotions and Experiences:
Betrayal, Bipolar, Depression, Holding onto The Past, Panic Disorder, Resignation, Rejection, Upheaval

Ingredients: Grapefruit, Lemon, Osmanthus, Melissa, and Siberian Fir

Did You Know? This essential oil is great for being used as part of a meditation, a spiritual practice, or during yoga.

Experience Enlightening Blend: Diffuse Enlightening Blend to promote feelings of confidence and calm when feeling stressed or in need of emotional balance.

Focus Blend

Use to Support These Positive Emotions and Experiences:
Attention, Clarity, Focus, Identity, Information Retention, Self-Assured

Use to Balance These Negative Emotions and Experiences:
ADD/ADHD, Autism/Aspergers, Conduct Disorder, Confusion, Difficulty with Transitions, Disconnected, Gender Dysphoria, Purposeless, Scattered, Willful--Excessive

Ingredients: Amyris Bark, Patchouli Leaf, Frankincense Resin, Lime Peel, Ylang Ylang Flower, Hawaiian Sandalwood Wood, Roman Chamomile Flower essential oils

Did You Know? The oil is a very synergistic blend of both grounding and relaxing oils and oils that enhance alertness and focus, making it an ideal blend for studying, work, learning, writing, or creating.

Experience Focus Blend: Apply Focus Blend on back of neck near hairline and rub in thoroughly to activate supportive aromatic chemistry for optimized brain function.

Gathering Blend

Use to Support These Positive Emotions and Experiences:
Comforted, Connected, Cooperative, Feeling "At Home" in Your Body, Nostalgia, Positive

Use to Balance These Negative Emotions and Experiences:
Broken Hearted, Disconnected, Distrusting, Lonely, Purposeless, Resentment

Ingredients: Cassia Bark, Clove, Nutmeg, Cinnamon, Cedarwood, Eucalyptus

Did You Know? Due to this blend having Clove, Cinnamon, and Cassia, it is very high in antioxidants and "feel good" aromatic molecules. Inhale it and feel the good vibes!

Experience Gathering Blend: Diffuse anytime you want to bring people together and get that holiday feel.

Grounding Blend

Use to Support These Positive Emotions and Experiences:
Body Positive, Confident, Flexible, Forgiving, Fulfilled, Grounded, Kind, Relaxed, Rooted, Trusting

Use to Balance These Negative Emotions and Experiences:
Aloof, Alzheimers, Anorexia, Anxiety, Autism/Aspergers, Bipolar, Body Dysmorphia, Controlling, Depersonalization, Disconnected, Distrusting, Embarrassed, Emptiness, Fear, Frustrated, Have to Be Right, Impatient, Insomnia, Isolated, Lonely, Materialistic, Negative Family Patterns, Night Terrors, Overstimulated, Panic Disorder, Parkinson's Disease, Perfectionism, Prideful, Reclusive, Rigid, Self Doubt, Self Righteous, Separation Anxiety Disorder, Social Anxiety, Stress, Tourette Syndrome, Unforgiving, Unstable, Upheaval, Weak Willed, Workaholism, Worry

Ingredients: Spruce Leaf, Ho Wood Leaf, Frankincense Resin, Blue Tansy Flower, Blue Chamomile Flower, and Osmanthus Flower essential oils in a base of Fractionated Coconut Oil.

Did you know? This blend helps helps to oxygenate the blood and increase blood flow.

Experience Grounding Blend: Apply over your heart or the bottom of your feet to relaxed and grounded.

Holiday Joyful Blend

Use to Support These Positive Emotions and Experiences:
Connected, Fulfilled, Momentum, Relaxed, Stable

Use to Balance These Negative Emotions and Experiences:
Debilitated, Emptiness, Fear, Isolated, Resentment, Unstable

Ingredients: Siberian Fir, Wild Orange, Clove Bud, Cinnamon Bark, Cassia, Douglas Fir, Nutmeg essential oils and Vanilla Absolute

Did you know? The oils in the blend are warming, familiar, and sweetly spicy and can make users feel like they're being enveloped in a warm hug.

Experience Holiday Joyful Blend: Diffuse Holiday Joyful Blend to create an environment of joyful connection and relaxed energy.

Holiday Peaceful Blend

Use to Support These Positive Emotions and Experiences:
Clarity, Freedom, Healthy Relationships, Light-Hearted, Peaceful, Positive, Relaxed, Self-Acceptance, Whole-Hearted

Use to Balance These Negative Emotions and Experiences:
Broken Hearted, Confusion, Critical, Depression, Guilt, Negative Family Patterns, Over Serious, Rejection, Shame, Stress

Ingredients: Siberian Fir, Douglas Fir, Himalayan Fir, Grapefruit, Frankincense, and Vetiver

Did you know? This blend has an abundance of tree oils (Siberian Fir, Douglas Fir, Himalayan Fir, Frankincense) which have a grounding energetic presence that can help users feel very comfortable in their own bodies.

Experience Holiday Peaceful Blend: Diffuse Holiday Peaceful Blend to promote feelings of being at ease and peace within your body.

Hopeful Blend

Use to Support These Positive Emotions and Experiences: Bravery, Hopeful, Organized, Peaceful, Self-Assuredness, Serenity

Use to Balance These Negative Emotions and Experiences: Frustrated, Overstimulated, Scattered, Self Doub

Ingredients: Bergamot, Ylang Ylang, Frankincense, Vanilla Bean Absolute

Did you know? These three essential oils in this blend are extremely nourishing to the emotional heart and soul of the user. This blend is a great go-to for almost any issue.

Experience Hopeful Blend: Apply Hopeful Blend on your heart and deeply inhale to allow the essential oils in this blend to uplift and comfort you emotionally.

Inspiring Blend

Use to Support These Positive Emotions and Experiences: Confidence, Connected, Fearless, Inspired, Healthy Boundaries, Levity, Purposeful, Soothed

Use to Balance These Negative Emotions and Experiences: Aloof, Bipolar, Broken Hearted, Codependency, Critical, Depression, Disconnected, Discouraged, Envy, Embarrassed, Hoarding, Isolated, Jealousy, Lack of Boundaries, Limiting Beliefs, Lonely, Over Serious, Parasitic Relationships, Purposeless, Reclusive, Resignation, Sadness, Scarcity

Ingredients: Fractionated Coconut Oil, Cardamom Seed, Cinnamon Bark, Ginger Rhizome, Clove Bud, Sandalwood Wood, Jasmine Flower Absolute, Vanilla Bean Absolute, Damiana Leaf.

Did you know? This blend has Cinnamon in it, which has been shown to enhance alertness while also reducing stress caused by workload--perfect for when inspiration strikes!

Experience Inspiring Blend: Apply Inspiring Blend over heart to enliven your energy and release any fears you may have about moving forward.

Invigorating Blend

Use to Support These Positive Emotions and Experiences:
Abundant, Comfort, Happiness, Involved, Joyful, Patient, Peaceful, Purposeful, Self Acceptance

Use to Balance These Negative Emotions and Experiences:
Aloof, Annoyed, Anorexia, Anxiety, Bipolar, Bulimia, Critical, Depersonalization, Depression, Disconnected, Embarrassed, Frustrated, Grief, Impatient, Isolated, Limiting Beliefs, Listless/Lost, Lonely, Materialistic, Overeating, Over Serious, Perfectionism, Purposeless, Reclusive, Resignation, Sadness, Scarcity, Separation Anxiety, Suicidal

Ingredients: Wild Orange Peel, Lemon Peel, Grapefruit Peel, Mandarin Peel, Bergamot Peel, Tangerine Peel, Clementine Peel essential oils and Vanilla Bean Absolute

Did you know? One of the most powerful ways to shift your mood is to inhale the aroma of an essential oil.

Experience Invigorating Blend: Diffuse Invigorating Blend to uplift your mood and create feelings of abundance.

Joyful Blend

Use to Support These Positive Emotions and Experiences:
Alive, Body Positivity, Connected, Divinely Directed, Enthusiastic, Happiness, Hopeful, Safe, Secure

Use to Balance These Negative Emotions and Experiences:
Abused, Aloof, Anorexia, Anxiety, Apathy, Bipolar, Critical, Depression, Disconnected, Embarrassed, Frustrated, Grief, Hoarding, Impatient, Isolated, Lost, Lonely, Perfectionism, Post Traumatic Stress Disorder, Purposeless, Reclusive, Resignation, Sadness, Suicidal, Trauma

Ingredients: Lavandin Flower, Tangerine Peel, Lavender Flower/Leaf, Amyris Bark, Clary Sage Flower/Leaf, Hawaiian Sandalwood Wood, Ylang Ylang Flower, Ho Wood Leaf, Osmanthus Flower, Lemon Myrtle Leaf, and Melissa Flower/Leaf essential oils

Did you know? This oil blend has flowers, fruit peels, bark, and leaves making it well-rounded.

Experience Joyful Blend: Diffuse to feel alive and enthused.

Kid's Courage Blend

Use to Support These Positive Emotions and Experiences:
Comfortable, Confident, Brave, Body Positive, Daring, Independent, Playful

Use to Balance These Negative Emotions and Experiences:
Autism/Aspergers, Body Dysmorphia, Codependency, Distrusting, Fear, Negative Family Patterns, Over Serious, Parasitic Relationships, Panic Disorder

Ingredients: Wild Orange, Amyris, Osmanthus, and Cinnamon in a base of Fractionated Coconut Oil

Did you know? Kid's Oil Blends are highly diluted and safe for kids, elderly, or anyone with sensitive skin. Even though these blends were formulated with kids in mind, they are great for adults too!

Experience Kid's Courage Blend: Apply Kid's Courage Blend to palms of hands and cup hands over nose, deeply inhaling aroma for 4 breaths.

Kid's Focus Blend

Use to Support These Positive Emotions and Experiences:
Attention, Comprehension, Confidence, Focus, Organized, Purposeful, Settled

Use to Balance These Negative Emotions and Experiences:
ADD/ADHD, Autism/Aspergers, Conduct Disorder, Confusion, Difficulty with Transitions, Disconnected, Gender Dysphoria, Purposeless, Scattered, Willful--Excessive

Ingredients: Vetiver, Clementine, Peppermint, and Rosemary in a base of Fractionated Coconut Oil

Did you know? Kid's Oil Blends are highly diluted and safe for kids, elderly, or anyone with sensitive skin. Even though these blends were formulated with kids in mind, they are great for adults too!

Experience Kid's Focus Blend: Apply Focus Blend to back of neck near hairline and rub in thoroughly to experience the centering, focusing effects of this oil.

Kid's Grounding Blend

Use to Support These Positive Emotions and Experiences:
Balance, Comfortable, Flexible, Forgiving, Grounded, Healthy Boundaries, Peaceful, Relaxed, Rested

Use to Balance These Negative Emotions and Experiences:
Autism/Aspergers, Bipolar, Body Dysmorphia, Fear, Frustrated, Have to Be Right, Insomnia, Negative Family Patterns, Night Terrors, Overstimulated, Panic Disorder, Prideful, Rigid, Self Righteous, Stress, Unforgiving, Unstable, Upheaval, Workaholism, Worry

Ingredients: Amyris Wood, Balsam Fir, Coriander, and Magnolia in Fractionated Coconut Oil

Did you know? Kid's Oil Blends are highly diluted and safe for kids, elderly, or anyone with sensitive skin. Even though these blends were formulated with kids in mind, they are great for adults too!

Experience Kid's Grounding Blend: Apply Kid's Grounding Blend to back of neck and bottoms of feet for a grounding, soothing effect on your mood.

Kid's Protective Blend

Use to Support These Positive Emotions and Experiences:
Confidence, Healthy Relationships, Inner Strength, Self Acceptance

Use to Balance These Negative Emotions and Experiences:
Bullying, Codependence, Parasitic Relationships, Weak Willed

Ingredients: Cedarwood, Litsea, Frankincense, and Rose in a base of Fractionated Coconut Oil

Did you know? Kid's Oil Blends are highly diluted and safe for kids, elderly, or anyone with sensitive skin. Even though these blends were formulated with kids in mind, they are great for adults too!

Experience Kid's Protective Blend: Apply Kid's Protective Blend to back of neck and chest to experience the protective properties of this essential oil in your surrounding environment.

Kid's Restful Blend

Use to Support These Positive Emotions and Experiences:
Being Enough, Body Positivity, Calm, Optimism, Peace, Positivity, Safety, Serenity

Use to Balance These Negative Emotions and Experiences:
Alzheimers, Autism/Aspergers, Bipolar Disorder, Body Dysmorphia, Conduct Disorder, Fear, Frustrated, Have to Be Right, Hate, Insomnia, Negative Family Patterns, Night Terrors, Over Stimulated, Panic Disorder, Parkinson's Disease, Prideful, Rigid, Scattered, Self-Righteous, Stress, Tourette Syndrome, Unforgiving, Unstable, Upheaval, Willful--Excessive, Workaholism, Worry

Ingredients: Cananga, Lavender, Buddha Wood, and Roman Chamomile essential oils in a base of Fractionated Coconut Oil

Did you know? Kid's Oil Blends are highly diluted and safe for kids, elderly, or anyone with sensitive skin. Even though these blends were formulated with kids in mind, they are great for adults too!

Experience Kid's Restful Blend: Apply Kid's Restful Blend to back of neck and chest to create a soothing, relaxed state of being.

Kid's Soothing Blend

Use to Support These Positive Emotions and Experiences:
Healthy Boundaries, Security, Surrender, Trust

Use to Balance These Negative Emotions and Experiences:
Betrayal, Codependency, Hoarding, Rejection, Stress

Ingredients: Lavender, Spearmint, Copaiba, and Zanthoxylum essential oil in a base of Fractionated Coconut Oil

Did you know? Kid's Oil Blends are highly diluted and safe for kids, elderly, or anyone with sensitive skin. Even though these blends were formulated with kids in mind, they are great for adults too!

Experience Kid's Soothing Blend: Apply Kid's Soothing Blend anywhere you feel tension or stress in the body caused by emotional distress (avoid eyes and genitals).

Massage Blend

Use to Support These Positive Emotions and Experiences:
Relaxed, Uplifting, Energizing, Clarity, Revitalized

Use to Balance These Negative Emotions and Experiences:
Stress, Fatigue, Tension, Uncertainty

Ingredients: Cypress Leaf, Peppermint Plant, Marjoram Leaf, Basil Leaf, Grapefruit Peel, Lavender Flower essential oils

Did you know? Peppermint is one of the main essential oils in this blend and helps to create a cooling sensation that can both reduce tension and also energize the body when applied topically.

Experience Massage Blend: Apply 1-2 drops to neck and shoulders for a minty, relaxing effect.

Metabolic Blend

Use to Support These Positive Emotions and Experiences:
Curbed Cravings, Peace, Rest, Self Acceptance

Use to Balance These Negative Emotions and Experiences:
Bulimia, Critical, Insomnia, Overeating

Ingredients: Grapefruit, Lemon, Peppermint, Ginger, and Cinnamon

Did you know? This blend helps internally by reducing cravings while also energizing and motivating it's users with a refreshing scent.

Experience Metabolic Blend: Place 2-3 drops of Metabolic Blend in 12oz of cold water and enjoy the spicy, warm taste of this blend and it's minty, citrus refreshment that helps to curb cravings and uplift the mood.

Monthly Blend

Use to Support These Positive Emotions and Experiences:
Self Confidence, Inner Peace, Serenity

Use to Balance These Negative Emotions and Experiences:
Lack of Libido, Moodiness, Self Doubt

Ingredients: Clary Sage, Lavender, Bergamot, Roman Chamomile, Cedarwood, Ylang Ylang, Geranium, Fennel, Carrot Seed, Palmarosa, and Vitex

Did you know? This blend works well as a perfume and can be worn throughout the month for balancing emotions everyday.

Experience Monthly Blend: Apply Monthly Blend over stomach, wrists, or back of neck to soothe an upset mood and promote inner peace.

Protective Blend

Use to Support These Positive Emotions and Experiences:
Happiness, Independence, Inner Strength, Fortitude

Use to Balance These Negative Emotions and Experiences:
Codependence, Parasitic Relationships, Weak Willed

Ingredients: Wild Orange Peel, Clove Bud, Cinnamon Leaf, Cinnamon Bark, Eucalyptus Leaf, and Rosemary Leaf/Flower essential oils

Did you know? The blend of essential oils in Protective Blend also make this a powerful immune system supporting oil and can be used to boost the immune system when needed as well.

Experience Protective Blend: Diffuse Protective Blend to create an energy of protection around you to help ward off parasitic energy from others as well as bacterial microbes in the environment.

Reassuring Blend

Use to Support These Positive Emotions and Experiences:
Accepting, Brain Health, Calm, Collected, Gratitude, Organized, Peaceful, Rest, Secure, Safety

Use to Balance These Negative Emotions and Experiences:
ADD, Anxiety, Autism, Betrayal, Bipolar, Codependency, Conduct Disorder, Controlling, Delusions, Distrusting, Embarrassed, Frustrated, Guilt, Hate, Impatient, Insomnia, Materialistic, Negative Family Patterns, Night Terrors, Obsessive Compulsive Disorder, Over Stimulated, Panic, Paranoia, Perfectionism, Pessimism, Phobias, Prideful, Psychosis, Regret, Resentment, Rejection, Rigid, Scattered, Schizophrenia, Self Righteous, Disorder, Shame, Stress, Willful

Ingredients: Vetiver Root, Lavender Flower, Ylang Ylang Flower, Frankincense Resin, Clary Sage Flower, Marjoram Leaf, Labdanum Leaf/Stalk, Spearmint Herb

Did you know? This blend was for kids but adults love it, too!

Experience Reassuring Blend: Apply over heart and back of neck to help balance almost any emotion.

Renewing Blend

Use to Support These Positive Emotions and Experiences:
Body Positivity, Comfort, Connected, Empathy, Forgiveness, Peace, Positivity, Relief, Relaxed, Self Acceptance, Whole

Use to Balance These Negative Emotions and Experiences:
Addiction, Anger, Annoyed, Anorexia, Apathy, Bereavement, Bitterness, Bulimia, Critical, Depersonalization, Despair, Disconnected, Discouraged, Embarrassed, Emptiness, Frustrated, Grief, Guilt, Hate, Isolated, Lonely, Negative Family Patterns, Overeating, Pessimism, Rage, Reclusive, Regret, Resentment, Sadness, Shame, Suicidal, Unforgiving, Upheaval

Ingredients: Spruce Leaf, Bergamot Peel, Juniper Berry Fruit, Myrrh Resin, Arborvitae Wood, Nootka Tree Wood, Thyme Leaf, Citronella Herb

Did you know? This oil helps with forgiving others.

Experience Renewing Blend: Diffuse to promote a healing environment for the heart and to move on with life.

Respiratory Blend

Use to Support These Positive Emotions and Experiences:
Capable, Energy, Lighthearted, Relief

Use to Balance These Negative Emotions and Experiences:
Addiction, Bereavement, Betrayal, Broken Hearted, Controlling, Despair, Embarrassed, Grief, Guilt, Holding onto The Past, Lack of Boundaries, Regret, Rejection, Shame

Ingredients: Laurel Leaf, Peppermint, Eucalyptus, Melaleuca, Lemon, Cardamom, Ravintsara, and Ravensara

Did you know? Cardamom and Eucalyptus are amazing for respiratory health.

Experience Respiratory Blend: Apply Respiratory Blend on chest and deeply inhale to relieve any emotional "weight".

Restful Blend

Use to Support These Positive Emotions and Experiences:
Being Enough, Body Positivity, Calm, Optimism, Peace, Positivity, Safety, Serenity

Use to Balance These Negative Emotions and Experiences:
Abused, ADD/ADHD, Alzheimers, Anxiety, Autism/Aspergers, Bipolar, Body Dysmorphia, Conduct Disorder, Controlling, Critical, Delusions, Difficulty with Transitions, Distrusting, Fear, Frustrated, Have to Be Right, Hate, Impatient, Insomnia, Materialistic, Negative Family Patterns, Night Terrors, Obsessive Compulsive Behavior, Over Stimulated, Panic Disorder, Paranoia, Parkinson's Disease, Perfectionism, Phobias, Prideful, Psychosis, Post Traumatic Stress, Rigid, Scattered, Schizophrenia, Self Righteous, Separation Anxiety Disorder, Social Anxiety, Stress, Trauma, Unforgiving, Unstable, Upheaval, Willful--Excessive, Workaholism

Ingredients: Lavender, Marjoram, Roman Chamomile, Ylang Ylang, Hawaiian Sandalwood, and Vanilla Bean

Did you know? Roman Chamomile is one of the most soothing and calming essential oils known to this world.

Experience Restful Blend: Apply Restful Blend to back of neck and over the heart to relax the body and release the mind from focusing on worrisome, anxious, or stressful thoughts.

Soothing Blend

Use to Support These Positive Emotions and Experiences:
Healthy Boundaries, Security, Surrender, Trust

Use to Balance These Negative Emotions and Experiences:
Betrayal, Codependency, Hoarding, Rejection, Stress

Ingredients: Wintergreen, Camphor, Peppermint, Ylang Ylang, Helichrysum, Blue Tansy, Blue Chamomile, and Osmanthus

Did you know? The first ingredient in this blend is Wintergreen. Wintergreen's main ingredient Methyl Salicylate has a very similar chemical structure to Aspirin so it is a wonderful pain-soothing essential oil to use for headaches or pains caused by stress or tense emotions.

Experience Soothing Blend: Apply Soothing Blend topically to neck, shoulders, or other areas of the body where tension is felt to provide soothing relief to any areas of stress or discomfort in the body (avoid eyes and genitals).

Steadying Blend

Use to Support These Positive Emotions and Experiences:
Calm, Grounded, Healthy Thoughts, Relaxed, Stable

Use to Balance These Negative Emotions and Experiences:
Delusions, Envy, Jealousy, Panic, Paranoia, Phobias, Psychosis, Schizophrenia, Unstable, Upheaval

Ingredients: Lavender, Cedarwood, Frankincense, Black Pepper, Cinnamon, Patchouli, Sandalwood, and Fractionated Coconut Oil

Did You Know? This essential oil is great for being used as part of a meditation, a spiritual practice, or during yoga.

Experience Steadying Blend: Apply Steadying Blend to bottom of feet to feel the balancing and grounding effects of this blend on your mood and circumstances.

Tension Blend

Use to Support These Positive Emotions and Experiences:
Healthy Boundaries, Security, Surrender, Trust

Use to Balance These Negative Emotions and Experiences:
Betrayal, Bitterness, Codependency, Hoarding, Rejection, Stress

Ingredients: Wintergreen Leaf, Lavender Flower, Peppermint Plant, Frankincense Resin, Cilantro Herb, Marjoram Leaf, Roman Chamomile Flower, Basil Leaf, and Rosemary Leaf essential oils

Did you know? This blend's first ingredient is Wintergreen. Wintergreen's main ingredient Methyl Salicylate has a very similar chemical structure to Aspirin so it is a wonderful pain-soothing essential oil to use for headaches or pains caused by stress or tense emotions.

Experience Tension Blend: Apply Tension Blend topically to neck, shoulders, or other areas of the body where tension is felt to provide soothing relief to any areas of stress or discomfort in the body (avoid eyes and genitals).

Topical Blend

Use to Support These Positive Emotions and Experiences:
Body Positivity, Healthy Boundaries, Cleansing, Protection

Use to Balance These Negative Emotions and Experiences:
Alert, Body Dysmorphia, Momentum, Parasitic Relationships, Stuck

Ingredients: Black Cumin Seed Oil, Ho Wood Leaf, Melaleuca Leaf, Litsea Berry, Eucalyptus Leaf, Geranium Plant essential oils

Did you know? This blend works wonderfully to shrink and clear up blemishes in a short period of time making it a wonderful addition to any emotional process that includes distress over appearance.

Experience Topical Blend: Apply Topical Blend to areas of concern and inhale it's spicy clean scent for a boost of alertness and momentum.

Uplifting Blend

Use to Support These Positive Emotions and Experiences:
Alert, Cheerful, Content, Energized, Happiness, Whole

Use to Balance These Negative Emotions and Experiences:
Alzheimers, Bipolar Disorder, Critical, Debilitated, Depression, Disconnected, Envy, Isolated, Jealousy, Limiting Beliefs, Lonely, Materialistic, Over Serious, Parkinson's Disease, Reclusive, Resignation, Sadness, Tourette Syndrome

Ingredients: Wild Orange Peel, Clove Bud, Star Anise Fruit/ Seed, Lemon Myrtle Leaf, Nutmeg Kernel, Vanilla Bean Extract, Ginger Rhizome, Cinnamon Bark, Zdravetz Herb

Did you know? Research shows that Uplifting Blend was the most pleasantly responded to out six emotional aromatherapy blends when diffused in a public setting. Participants reported elevated mood across the board when this oil was diffused.

Experience Uplifting Blend: Diffuse Uplifting Blend to banish any bad moods or grumpy attitudes and experience the calming and uplifting effects of this sweet citrus aroma.

Bibliography and Endnotes

For bibliography and endnotes visit:
www.feelinggoodwithoils.com/notes

For questions or to share a testimonial please email:
FeelingGoodWithOils@gmail.com